VEGETARIAN
Recipes

Nita Mehta
B.Sc. (Home Science), M.Sc. (Food and Nutrition)
Gold Medalist

SNAB
Excellence in Books

Nita Mehta's
VEGETARIAN Recipes

© Copyright 2007-2011 **SNAB** Publishers Pvt Ltd

WORLD RIGHTS RESERVED. The contents—all recipes, photographs and drawings are original and copyrighted. No portion of this book shall be reproduced, stored in a retrieval system or transmitted by any means, electronic, mechanical, photocopying, recording or otherwise, without the written permission of the publishers.

While every precaution is taken in the preparation of this book, the publisher and the author assume no responsibility for errors or omissions. Neither is any liability assumed for damages resulting from the use of information contained herein.

TRADEMARKS ACKNOWLEDGED. Trademarks used, if any, are acknowledged as trademarks of their respective owners. These are used as reference only and no trademark infringement is intended upon.

3rd Print 2011
ISBN 978-81-7869-142-8

Food Styling and Photography: **SNAB**

Layout and Laser Typesetting :

N.I.T.A. ☎ 23252948
National Information Technology Academy
3A/3, Asaf Ali Road
New Delhi-110002

Distributed by :
NITA MEHTA BOOKS
Distributors & Publishers
NITA MEHTA BOOKS
3A/3, Asaf Ali Road, New Delhi - 02

Distribution Centre:
D16/1, Okhla Industrial Area, Phase-I,
New Delhi-110020
Tel.: 26813199, 26813200

Printed in India

Contributing Writers :
Anurag Mehta
Tanya Mehta
Subhash Mehta

Editors :
Sangeeta
Sunita

Published by :

SNAB
Excellence in Books
Publishers Pvt. Ltd.
3A/3 Asaf Ali Road,
New Delhi - 110002
Tel: 23252948, 23250091

Editorial and Marketing office:
E-159, Greater Kailash-II, N.Delhi-48
nitamehta@nitamehta.com
*Website:*http://www.nitamehta.com

Recipe Development & Testing:

Nita Mehta Foods - R & D Centre
3A/3, Asaf Ali Road, New Delhi-110002
E-143, Amar Colony, Lajpat Nagar-IV
New Delhi-110024

Rs. 89/-

INTRODUCTION

*M*ore and more people are discovering the joy of Vegetarian Cooking – and also the enormous health benefits. Vegetarian food is easy on the digestion and prevents disease. A generous use of products such as soya, cheese, paneer, nuts and yogurt ensures the protein content of the diet.

This book is packed with fresh, light and innovative recipes with fabulous tastes and textures, drawing from Indian, Chinese and Continental cuisines. Here is proof that the Vegetarian Way is not only nutritious and quick, it is also deliciously varied and exciting!

Nita Mehta

CONT

Introduction 3

Curries 6
Dhania Paneer 7
Lajawab Baingan Aur Mirch 10
Gobhi ke kofte 13
Gatte ke Subzi 16

Shahi Paneer 19
Dal Makhani 22
Malai Matar Paneer 24
Vegetable Korma 26

Dry & Masala Dishes 29
Mili-Juli-Subzi 30
Saboot Phool Dilkhush 33
Aloo Bhare Karele 36

Bhindi with Moongphali 39
Baingan Achaari 42
Sukhe Matar Mushroom 45

Baked Dishes 48
Potatoes Baked in Mustard Sauce 49
Baked Vegetables 52

Veggie and Bean Casserole 55
Stacked Corn Pancakes 58

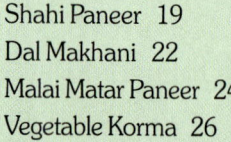

E N T S

Chinese 61

American Chopsuey with Sweet & Sour Vegetables 62
Cottage Cheese in Hot Garlic Sauce 65
Stir-fried Beans with Tofu/Paneer 68

Haka Noodles 71
Peanut Fried Rice 74
Chilli Cauliflower 76

Snacks 78

Super veggie Pizza 79
Pan-Fried Chinese Tikkas 82
Matar Makhane ke Kebab 85

Palak Pakoras 88
Pasta in Quick Tomato Sauce 90
Tikka Parantha Sandwich 92

Desserts 96

Bread and Paneer Pudding 97
Mango Kulfi 100

Glossary of Names/Terms 102
International Conversion Guide 103

Curries

Dhania Paneer

Make a paste of coriander leaves, stir into a paste of cashew nuts and dilute with milk to make the gravy for this delectable paneer curry!

Serves 4

200 gm paneer - cut into 1" square pieces

2 tbsp cashewnuts (*kaju*) - soak in warm water for 10 minutes & grind to a paste

4 tbsp oil, 1 big onion - finely chopped

1" piece ginger & 8-10 flakes garlic - crushed to a paste or 2 tsp ginger-garlic paste

½ tsp red chilli powder, ½ tsp garam masala

1 tsp salt, or to taste, 1 tsp coriander (*dhania*) powder

2 tbsp chopped coriander, 1 cup milk

CORIANDER PASTE

¾ cup chopped coriander

2 green chillies

1 tbsp fennel (*saunf*), ½ cup milk

1. Soak kaju in a little warm water for 10-15 minutes. Drain. Grind in a mixer to a very smooth paste using about 2 tbsp water.

2. Grind all the ingredients for the coriander paste to make a thin paste in a mixer- grinder.

3. Heat 4 tbsp oil in a kadhai and add the chopped onions. Fry till golden.

4. Add the ginger- garlic paste, stir for few seconds.

5. Reduce heat, add the prepared coriander paste. Cook for 2 minutes.

6. On medium flame, add red chilli powder, garam masala, salt and dhania powder.

7. Add the prepared kaju paste. Mix well. Keep scraping sides if masala sticks to the sides/bottom of the kadhai. Stir till masala leaves oil.

8. Add ½ cup of water. Boil, stirring at intervals. Remove from fire. Let the gravy cool down a little.

9. Add milk, mix well. Add paneer and return to fire and cook stirring continuously on low heat for 3-4 minutes. Serve hot, garnished with chopped coriander.

Lajawab Baingan Aur Mirch

The base of this famous dish is made with sesame seeds, peanuts and coconut along with a sharp taste of tamarind – brinjals and green chillies are fried, then simmered in the gravy.

Serves 4

4-5 large, thick green chillies (*achaari hari mirch*)

6 brinjals (small thin variety) - sliced to get rounds and sprinkled with salt

3 onions - cut into 4 pieces and boiled in 1 cup water for 4-5 minutes till soft

a lemon sized ball of tamarind (*imli*), 5 tbsp oil

½ tsp mustard seeds (*sarson*), ½ tsp onion seeds (*kalonji*), 3 tbsp fresh cream

GRIND TOGETHER TO A SMOOTH PASTE

2 tbsp sesame seeds (*til*), 2 tbsp peanuts (*moongphali*)

2 tsp desiccated coconut (coconut powder), optional

6 flakes garlic, 1½" piece of ginger, 2 tsp coriander powder

1 tsp cumin seeds (*jeera*), ½ tsp red chilli powder, 1 tsp salt

1 tsp lemon juice

1. Cut onions roughly and boil till soft. Drain and grind to a paste. Keep boiled onion paste aside.
2. Wash tamarind. Put in a bowl with 1½ cups hot water. Mash. Soak for 10 minutes. Strain to extract juice.
3. Grind the sesame seeds, peanuts, coconut, ginger, garlic, coriander, jeera, red chilli powder, salt and lemon juice to a paste with a little water. Keep aside.
4. Pat dry the brinjals sprinkled with salt on a clean kitchen towel.
5. Heat 5-6 tbsp oil in pan. Reduce heat and fry the green chillies for 1½ minutes. Remove the chillies from the oil and keep aside. In the same oil, add the brinjals. Fry turning sides on medium heat till they change colour and turn brownish. Check with a knife and remove from oil when they turn soft.
6. For gravy, heat 2 tbsp oil and add kalonji and sarson. Wait for ½ minute till they crackle, add boiled onion paste. Fry till onions turn light golden.
7. Add the freshly ground peanut-sesame paste and fry for 1-2 minutes.
8. Add ½ cup water in the pan and stir and then pour strained tamarind juice into the pan. Mix. Add fried chillies and baingan. Boil and simmer for 7-8 minutes on low heat. Check salt. Remove from fire. Serve hot.

Gobhi ke kofte

*Grated cauliflower or broccoli is bound with boiled potato and shaped into koftas.
The gravy is a careful blend of tomatoes, milk and cream.*

Serves 4-6

1 medium cauliflower or broccoli - grated finely along with tender stalks (2 cups grated)

1 potato - boiled and grated, ½ tsp butter

2 tbsp roasted peanuts (*moongphali*) - crushed coarsely

¼ tsp coarsely crushed peppercorns (*saboot kali mirch*)

½ tsp salt, ¼ tsp garam masala, ¼ tsp dried mango powder (*amchoor*), 1½ tbsp cornflour

a pinch of baking powder, 1 cheese cube (20 gm) - cut into 10 pieces

GRAVY

5 tomatoes - pureed in a mixer or 1 cup ready-made tomato puree

3 tbsp oil, 1 tsp cumin seeds (*jeera*), 1" piece ginger - grated, 1 tsp ginger paste

1¼ tsp salt, ¾ tsp garam masala, 1½ tsp coriander (*dhania*) powder

½ tsp red chilli powder, 4 tbsp chopped coriander

1 cup water, 1 cup milk, ¼-½ cup cream or fresh *malai*

1. Grate the cauliflower or broccoli florets and the tender stems very finely.
2. Heat ½ tbsp butter in a pan. Add chopped broccoli and ¼ tsp salt. Stir on medium heat for 3-4 minutes. Remove from heat.
3. Grate the potato well. Add peanuts, crushed peppercorns, salt, garam masala, amchoor, cornflour, baking powder and cooked broccoli to the potato.
4. Make balls of the potato-broccoli mixture. Flatten a ball and put a small piece of cheese in it. Make a ball again. Deep fry 2-3 balls at a time till golden.
5. To prepare the gravy, heat oil. Add jeera. Let it turn golden.
6. When golden, add ginger shreds and ginger paste. Mix well.
7. Add tomato puree. Add salt, garam masala, dhania powder and red chilli powder. Cook for 5-8 minutes, till puree turns dry and oil separates
8. Add coriander. Add enough water to get a thick gravy. Boil. Cook on low heat for 4-5 minutes. Remove from fire. Cool.
9. To serve, add enough milk to the cold gravy stirring continuously. Add koftas. Keep on low heat and stir continuously till just about to boil. Add cream and remove from fire after 2-3 seconds. Serve.

Gatte ke Subzi

Vegetarian cooking is more than just vegetables: Learn to make gatte from gram flour (besan). After steaming, they are simmered in a light tomato gravy.

Serves 4-5

¾ cup gram flour (besan)

¼ tsp baking soda (mitha soda), ½ tsp ginger-green chilli paste

¼ tsp carom seeds (ajwain), ¼ tsp saunf (fennel) - crushed

½ tsp - salt, haldi, red chilli, dhania and garam masala

2 tbsp curd, 1 tbsp oil

CURRY

3 tbsp oil, 2 laung (cloves)

1 tsp jeera, 1 moti elaichi - crushed

¼ tsp haldi, ½ tsp red chilli powder

2 large tomatoes - puree in a mixer & strain

½ tsp ginger-chilli paste, ¾ cup curd mixed with 2 tsp besan

1. Sift besan and soda. Add ginger chilli paste, ajwain, saunf, spices and just enough curd to get a very soft dough. Mix well. Mix 1 tbsp oil and knead again. Make 4 balls. With the help of oil smeared on your hands, roll out thin fingers 3"-4" long, like cylinders.

2. Boil 5 cups of water. Keep the gattae in a steamer basket or a stainless steel round strainer and keep the strainer on the pan of boiling water and cover with a lid.

3. Steam gatte for 5-7 minutes. Let them cool. Later cut them into rounds of ½" thickness. Keep aside.

4. For curry, blend curd and besan in a mixer till very smooth. Add 1 cup water. Puree tomatoes and strain them to get a smooth puree.

5. Heat 2 tbsp oil, add laung, jeera, moti elaich, haldi & red chilli powder. Stir. Add tomato puree & ginger-chilli paste. Cook for 3 minutes till dry & oil separates.

6. Reduce heat. Add curd with besan and water. Stir constantly, on low heat to bring it to a boil. Simmer for 6-8 minutes.

7. Add gatte. Cook for 1-2 minutes. Serve hot garnished with hara dhania.

Shahi Paneer

Now make this five-star special in your own kitchen – the red, tomato-cream gravy has a gentle touch of fenugreek leaves and cardamom.

Serves 4

250 gm paneer - cut into 1" cubes

5 large (500 gm) tomatoes - each cut into 4 pieces

2 tbsp desi ghee or butter and 2 tbsp oil, ½ tsp cumin seeds (*jeera*)

4-5 flakes garlic and 1" piece ginger - ground to a paste (1½ tsp ginger-garlic paste)

1 tbsp dried fenugreek leaves (*kasoori methi*)

1 tsp tomato ketchup, 2 tsp coriander (*dhania*) powder

½ tsp garam masala, 1 tsp salt, or to taste, ½ tsp red chilli powder, preferably *degi mirch*

seeds of 1 green cardamom (*chhoti elaichi*)

½-1 cup milk, approx., ½ cup cream (optional)

CASHEW PASTE

3 tbsp cashewnuts (*kaju*) - soaked in ¼ cup warm water for 15 minutes and ground to a very fine paste

1. Boil tomatoes in ½ cup water. Simmer for 5 minutes on low heat till soft. Remove from fire and cool. Grind tomatoes along with water to a smooth puree.

2. Heat oil and ghee or butter in a kadhai. Reduce heat. Add jeera. When it turns golden, add ginger garlic paste.

3. When paste starts to change colour, add the above tomato puree and cook till absolutely dry. Add kasoori methi and tomato ketchup.

4. Add masalas - dhania powder, garam masala, salt and red chilli powder. Mix well for a few seconds. Cook till oil separates.

5. Add cashew paste. Mix well for 2 minutes. Add chhoti elaichi powder.

6. Add ½ cup water. Boil. Simmer on low heat for 4-5 minutes. Reduce heat. Add the paneer cubes. Keep aside to cool till serving time.

7. At serving time, add enough milk to the cold paneer masala to get a thick curry, mix gently. (Remember to add milk only after the masala cools down, to prevent the milk from curdling. After adding milk, heat curry on low heat.)

8. Heat on low heat, stirring continuously till just about to boil. Add cream, keeping the heat very low and stirring continuously. Remove from fire immediately. Sprinkle 1 tsp kasoori methi. Serve hot.

Dal Makhani

This traditional dal cooked to a creamy, rich consistency has fans all over the world.

Serves 4-5

1 cup whole black beans (*urad saboot*)
2 tbsp desi ghee, 1½ tsp salt, 5 cups of water
1 cup ready-made tomato puree
¼ tsp nutmeg (*jaiphal*) powder, ½ tsp garam masala
1½ tbsp dry fenugreek leaves (*kasoori methi*)
2-3 tbsp butter, preferably white

GRIND TO A PASTE
2 dry, whole red chillies
- deseeded & soaked for 10 minutes
1 tsp chopped ginger, 6-8 flakes garlic

ADD LATER
½ cup milk mixed with ½ cup cream

1. Wash the dal, and soak in warm water for at least 2-3 hours.
2. Drain water and wash well. Pressure cook dal with 5 cups water, 2 tbsp ghee, salt and ginger-garlic-chilli paste. After the first whistle, keep on low flame for 30 minutes. Remove from fire.
3. After the pressure drops, mash the hot dal a little.
4. To the dal in the cooker, add tomato puree, kasoori methi, garam masala and jaiphal powder. Add butter. Simmer on medium flame for 30 minutes, stirring dal occasionally. Remove from fire. Keep aside to cool till the time of serving.
5. At serving time, add milk mixed with cream to the dal. Keep dal on fire and bring to a boil on low heat, stirring constantly. Mix very well with a karchhi. Simmer for 2 minutes more, to get the right colour and smoothness. Remove from fire. Serve by dropping cream with a tsp in a circle on the hot dal.

Malai Matar Paneer

Serves 3-4

100 gm cottage cheese (*paneer*) - cut into small, ½" cubes, 1 cup boiled or frozen peas

½ stick cinnamon (*dalchini*), 2 cardamoms (*moti elaichi*), 3-4 cloves (*laung*)

1 tbsp cashewnuts (*kaju*), 2 tbsp oil, 1 large onion - ground to a paste

¼ tsp white pepper powder, ½ cup (75 gm) cream (*malai*)-beat with ½ cup milk till smooth

4 tbsp dry fenugreek leaves (*kasoori methi*), salt to taste, a pinch of sugar, ½ cup milk

1. Crush together dalchini, laung and seeds of moti elaichi on a chakla-belan. Keep the masala aside. Grind cashewnuts separately to a fine powder.

2. Heat oil. Add ground onion and cook on low heat till very light golden and oil separates. Add the crushed masala and pepper powder. Cook for a few seconds.

3. Add kasoori methi and malai, cook on low heat for 2-3 minutes till malai dries up slightly. Add boiled peas and paneer.

4. Add powdered cashewnuts and cook for a few seconds. Add enough milk to get a thick gravy. Add salt and sugar to taste. Remove from fire. Serve.

Vegetable Korma

A delicious korma, brimming with vegetables & paneer cubes – extraordinary gravy of poppy seeds, coconut & yogurt.

Serves 4

6-8 florets of cauliflower - deep-fried till golden, ½ cup shelled peas (*matar*)

2 slices of tinned pineapple - cut into 1" pieces, 2 small carrots - cut into round slices

4-5 French beans - cut into ½" diagonal pieces

2 onions - chopped finely, 4 tbsp oil

¼ tsp turmeric (*haldi*) powder, ½ tsp garam masala, 2 tsp salt

GRIND TOGETHER (CASHEW-CURD PASTE)

4 tsp poppy seeds (*khus-khus*) - soaked in warm water for 30 minutes and drained

¾ cup curd, 2 tbsp cashews (*kaju*), 2 tbsp grated coconut (fresh or desiccated)

2 whole dry red chillies, ½" piece ginger, 3-4 flakes garlic

2 tsp coriander seeds (*saboot dhania*)

seeds of 2-3 green cardamoms (*chhoti elaichi*)

1. Soak khus-khus, kaju, coconut, red chillies, ginger, garlic, saboot dhania and chhoti elaichi with little water. Keep aside for 15 minutes.
2. Drain and grind together to a paste along with curd. Keep aside the paste.
3. Deep-fry cauliflower florets till golden.
4. Heat 4 tbsp oil. Add chopped onions. Cook till onions turn golden. Add haldi. Stir to mix well.
5. Add the prepared cashew-curd paste. Cook on low heat for 3-4 minutes.
6. Add beans, peas and carrots. Stir for 2 minutes.
7. Add 1 cup water or enough to get a thick gravy. Boil.
8. Add garam masala and salt. Simmer for 5 minutes.
9. Add cauliflower and pineapple. Boil for 1 minute. Serve hot.

Note: Do not use fresh pineapple without boiling the pieces in some water for 4-5 minutes. It can make the korma bitter!

Dry & Masala Dishes

Mili-Juli-Subzi

The colour and look of each vegetable is well preserved.
An onion-tomato coating adds a zesty thrill!

Serves 4-6

1 big potato - peeled, scooped to form small balls (about 12-13 balls) or cut into ½" pieces

200 gm (1 packet) baby cabbage or brussel sprouts (15- 20 pieces) - trim the stalk end or ½ of a small cabbage - cut into 1" pieces

100 gm baby corn (7-8) - keep whole if small or cut into 2 pieces if big, ¼ cup peas (*matar*)

6-7 French beans - cut into ¼" pieces (½ cup), 1 carrot - cut into round slices

12-15 baby onions or 4 regular onions of small size - each cut into 4 pieces

15 cherry tomatoes or 2 regular small tomatoes - cut into 4, remove pulp, ¼ tsp turmeric (*haldi*)

1 tsp salt, ½ tsp red chilli powder, 6 tbsp oil, ½ tsp garam masala, ½ tsp paprika (*degi mirch*)

ONION PASTE

1 onion, 2 cloves (*laung*), 2 green cardamom (*chhoti elaichi*)

TOMATO PASTE

¼ cup yogurt (*dahi*), 2 tomatoes - put in boiling hot water for 3-4 minutes & peeled (blanched)

1. Make balls of a big potato with the help of a scooper.

2. Boil 7 cups water with 2 tsp salt. Add potato balls. Boil for 3-4 minutes till soft. Add cabbage, baby corns, peas, beans and carrots. Boil for a minute. Remove from fire. Strain, put in cold water and strain again.

3. Heat 3 tbsp oil. Add onions. Saute for 2 minutes till soft. Add tomatoes. Stir.

4. Add all the vegetables. Sprinkle ½ tsp salt. Saute for 1 minute. Keep aside.

5. Grind all the ingredients of onion paste to a smooth paste. Keep aside.

6. Grind all the ingredients of tomato paste to a smooth paste. Keep aside.

7. For masala, heat remaining 3 tbsp oil, add onion paste. Cook till light brown. Add haldi.

8. Add tomato paste. Stir for 5-10 minutes or till oil separates.

9. Add salt and red chilli powder. Cook till dry and oil separates.

10. Add ¾ cup water, ½ tsp garam masala and degi mirch. Cook for ½ a minute.

11. Add stir fried vegetables. Mix well for 2-3 minutes. Serve hot.

Saboot Phool Dilkhush

Serves 6-8

2 very small whole cauliflowers

5-6 tbsp oil, 3 onions - ground to a paste, 3 tomatoes - roughly chopped

2 tsp chopped ginger, seeds of 1 cardamom (*moti elaichi*)

3-4 peppercorns (*saboot kali mirch*) and 2 cloves (*laung*), 2 tbsp curd - beat well till smooth

½ tsp red chilli powder, ½ tsp garam masala, ½ tsp turmeric (*haldi*)

½ tsp dried mango powder (*amchoor*), ½ tsp salt, or to taste, ¼ cup boiled peas - to garnish

1. Remove stems of cauliflowers. Boil 6 cups water with 2 tsp salt. Put the whole cauliflowers in it. When the water starts to boil again, remove from fire. Leave them in hot water for 10 minutes. Remove from water and refresh in cold water. Wipe dry on a clean kitchen towel.

2. Heat 5-6 tbsp oil in a pan. Put both cauliflowers with flower side down in oil. Cover and cook on medium flame, turning occasionally till the cauliflowers get patches of dark brown colour here and there. Remove from oil. Keep aside.

3. Heat ½ tbsp oil in a clean kadhai. Add moti elaichi, saboot kali mirch and laung. After a minute add tomatoes and ginger. Cook for 4-5 minutes till they turn soft. Grind the cooked tomatoes to a paste. Reserved.

4. Heat 3½ tbsp oil. Add onion paste. Cook till onions turn golden brown.

5. Add reserved tomato paste. Cook for 3-4 minutes on low flame till turns dry.

6. Add well beaten curd. Cook till masala turns reddish again.

7. Reduce heat. Add red chilli powder, garam masala, haldi, amchoor and salt. Cook for 1 minute. Add ¼ cup water to get a thick, dry masala. Boil. Cook for 1 minute on low flame. Remove from fire.

8. Insert a little masala in between the florets of the fried cauliflower, especially from the back.

9. To serve, arrange cauliflowers on a platter. Add ¼ cup water to the masala to make it a masala gravy. Boil. Add ½ tsp salt or to taste. Pour over the arranged cauliflowers. Heat in a microwave or a preheated oven. Alternately, heat the cauliflower in a kadhai in 1 tbsp oil at the time of serving. Heat the masala gravy separately. Pour the hot masala gravy over the arranged cauliflowers.

10. Sprinkle some boiled peas on it and on the sides. Serve.

Aloo Bhare Karele

Bitter gourds are stuffed with mashed potatoes and given a sweet (raisins) and sour (amchoor) touch – guaranteed to increase the number of admirers of this unique vegetable.

Serves 6-8

500 gm (8-9) medium bitter gourds (*karelas*)

FILLING

2 large potatoes - boiled & mashed coarsely, ½ tsp cumin seeds (*jeera*)

½ tsp mustard seeds (*sarson*), 1 onion - sliced finely, ¼ tsp turmeric (*haldi*) powder

½ tsp chilli powder, salt to taste, ¾ tsp garam masala

1½ tbsp raisins (*kishmish*) - soaked in water for 15 minutes, 1 tsp til, 1 tomato - chopped

2 green chillies - deseeded & chopped, 2 - 3 tbsp chopped coriander

1 tsp dried mango powder (*amchoor*)

1. Peel karelas, keeping the stalks intact. Slit. Remove all seeds if they are hard, if not too hard, remove some to make place for the stuffing. Rub salt inside and on the surface of karelas. Keep aside for at least 1 hour.

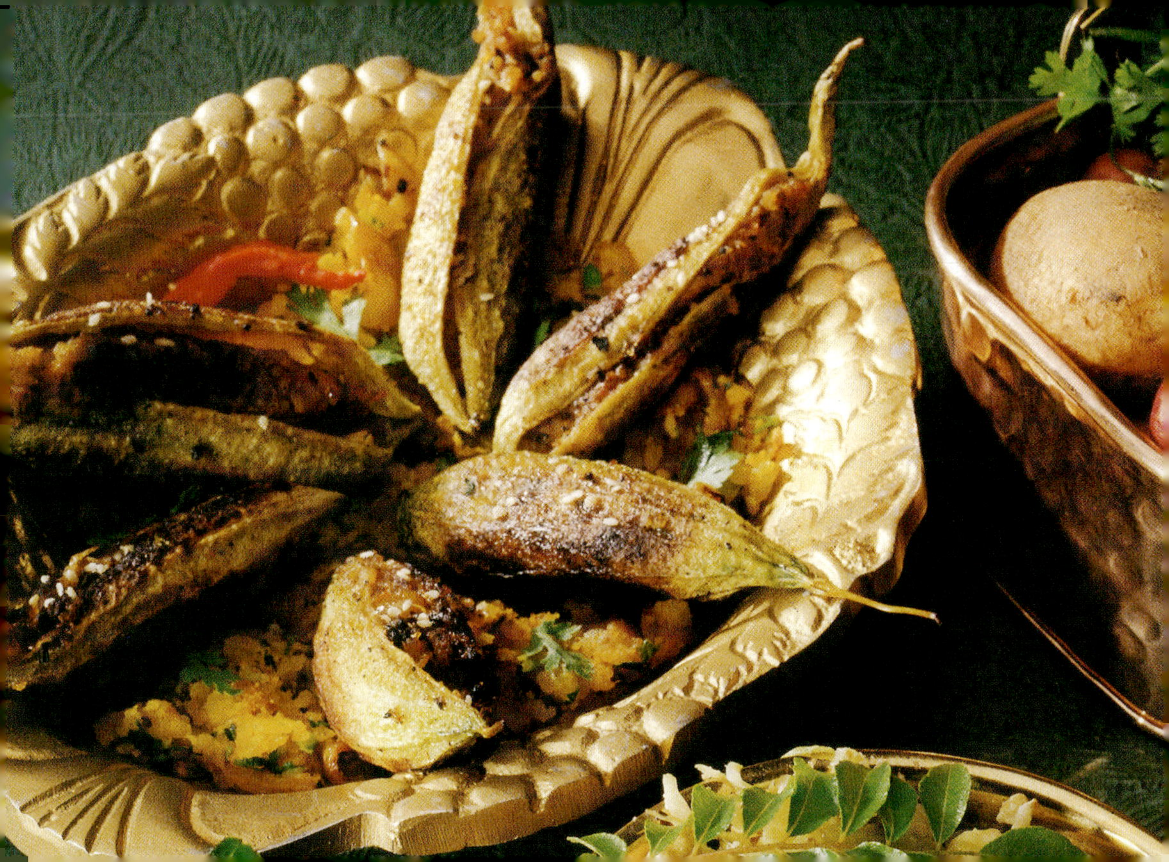

2. Heat 3 tbsp oil in a kadhai. Reduce flame. Add jeera and sarson. Fry till jeera changes colour.

3. Add onions and fry till transparent. Add salt, red chilli powder, garam masala and haldi powder.

4. Add kishmish and til. Stir for a minute.

5. Add tomato, green chillies and coriander. Stir-fry for 1- 2 minutes.

6. Add the roughly mashed potatoes and amchoor. Stir-fry for 4-5 minutes on low flame. Remove from fire.

7. Squeeze the karelas, wash a few times.

8. Fill 1-2 tbsp of potato stuffing in each karela. Press to join the sides.

9. Heat 4-5 tbsp oil in a big flat bottomed kadhai. Put in the karelas, one by one gently. Cook uncovered on medium flame for 10-12 minutes, turning them occasionally, to brown them evenly. Cover and cook further for 5 minutes or till soft.

10. Remove from fire and drain out the extra oil. Serve sprinkled with some roasted til.

Bhindi with Moongphali

*A quick and crisp combination of fried lady fingers & peanuts –
this recipe will soon become a family favourite!*

Serves 4

300 gm lady fingers (*bhindi*) - cut diagonally into 1" long pieces

½ cup peanuts - deep fried

3-4 flakes garlic - crushed roughly

1 onion - chopped finely

1 tomato - chopped finely

1 tomato - pureed in a mixer

1½ tsp coriander (*dhania*) powder

½ tsp garam masala

¾-1 tsp salt

½ tsp red chilli powder

2 tsp tomato chilli sauce (maggi), oil to fry

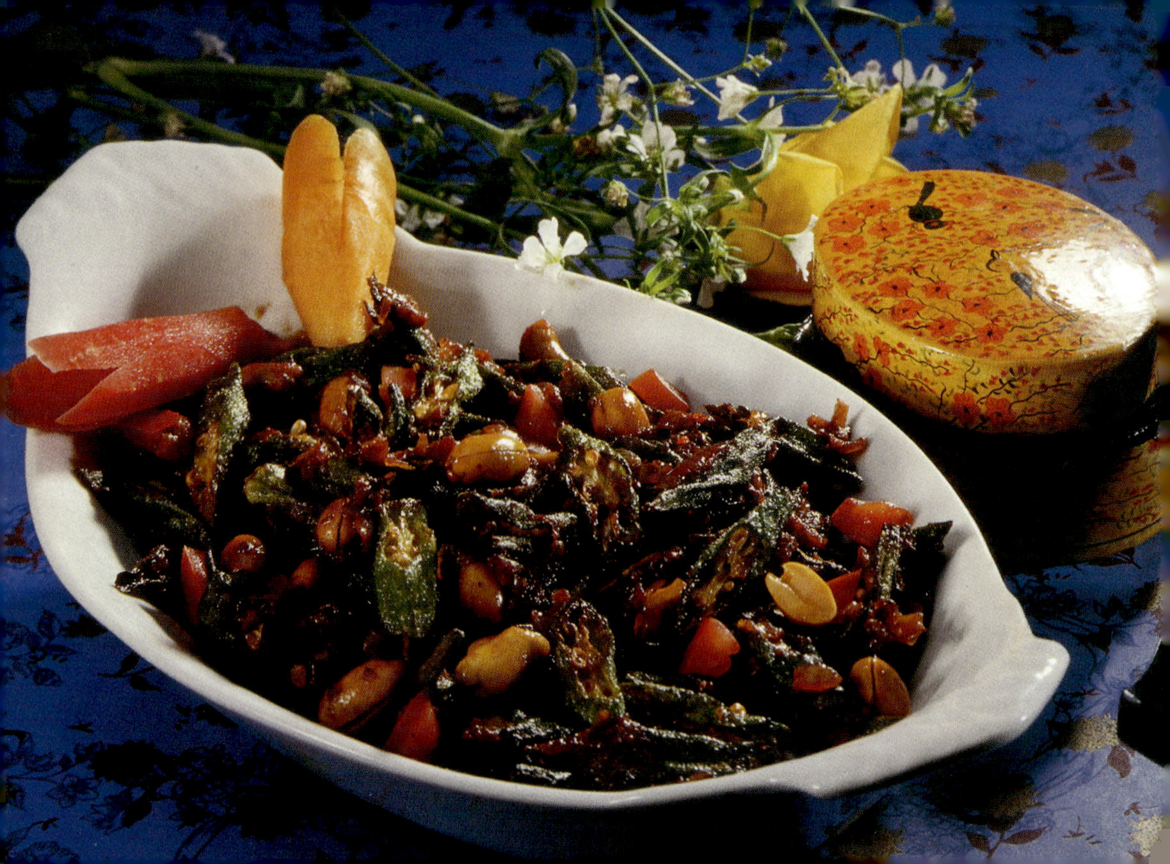

1. Wash bhindi. Wipe with a clean kitchen towel. Cut the tip of the head of each bhindi. Leave the pointed end as it is. Cut diagonally to get 1" pieces.

2. Heat some oil for deep-frying in a kadhai to medium hot temperature. Add half of the bhindi and fry on medium flame for about 5 minutes till it gets cooked. Remove from oil on a paper napkin.

3. Fry the second batch of bhindi also.

4. In the same oil deep-fry the peanuts also till golden. Drain on a paper napkin.

5. Remove all the oil from the kadhai. Heat 2 tbsp oil again in the kadhai.

6. Reduce flame. Add garlic and fry till it changes colour. Add onion and fry till golden brown.

7. Add chopped tomato, cook for 4-5 minutes till it leaves oil.

8. Add fresh tomato puree, dhania powder, garam masala, salt, red chilli powder and tomato chilli sauce.

9. Stir for a minute on low flame. Add the fried peanuts and fried bhindi. Stir for a few minutes. Serve hot.

Baingan Achaari

Fried brinjals are stirred into a light masala that is flavoured with the traditional achaari (pickling) spices – saunf, kalonji, methi, rai.

Serves 4

750 gm (7-8) brinjals of long thin variety

½ kg tomatoes - chopped finely

2 tsp ginger or garlic paste

15-20 curry leaves, 2 tbsp oil

½ tsp red chilli powder

1 tbsp coriander (*dhania*) powder

½ tsp turmeric (*haldi*), 1 tsp salt, or to taste

COLLECT TOGETHER

a pinch of asafoetida (*hing*)

1 tsp fennel (*saunf*), ½ tsp onion seeds (*kalonji*)

½ tsp fenugreek seeds (*methi dana*), 1 tsp mustard seeds (*rai*)

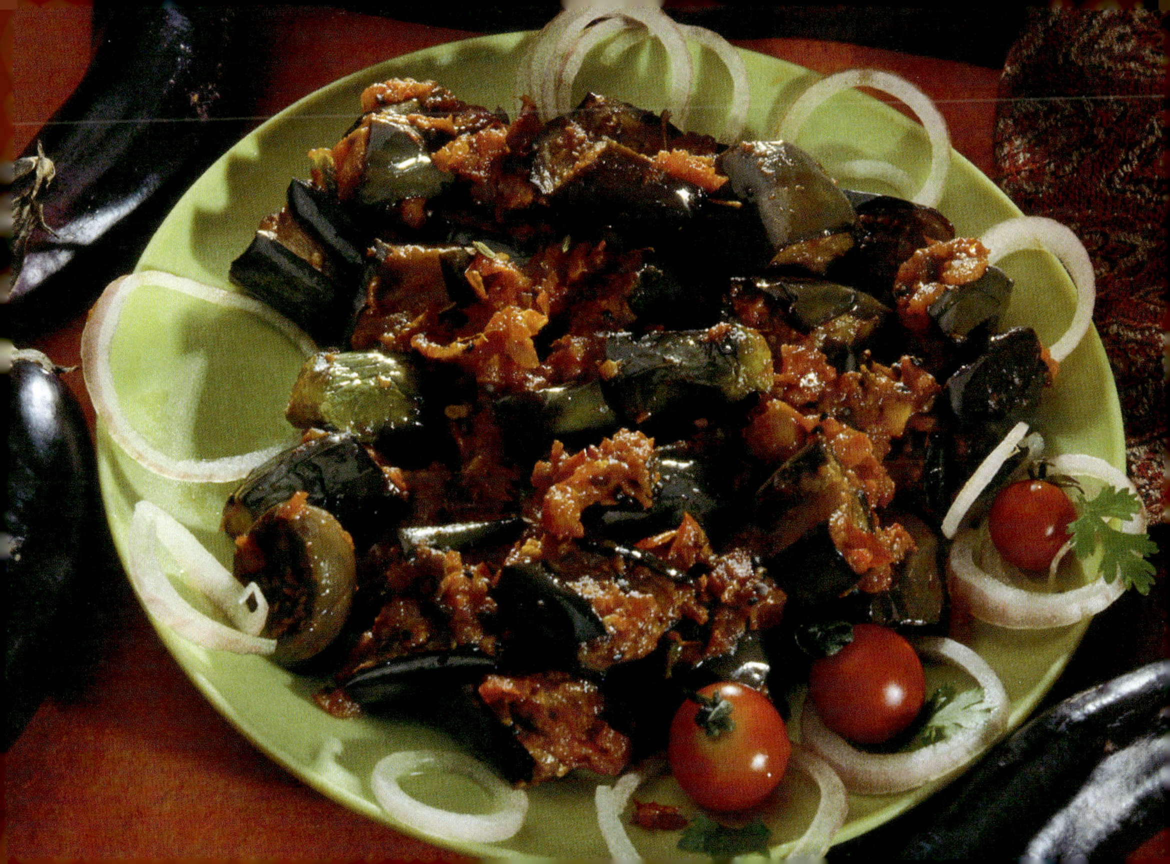

1. Cut brinjals into half lengthwise and then into 1" pieces.
2. Deep fry brinjals till light brown.
3. Heat 2 tbsp oil and add ginger or garlic paste. Add curry patta and stir fry for a minute.
4. Reduce heat. Add all collected ingredients together – hing, saunf, kalonji, methi dana and rai. Stir till methi dana turns brown.
5. Add haldi, red chilli powder, dhania powder and salt. Stir for 30 seconds.
6. Add chopped tomatoes and stir for about 7-8 minutes or till oil separates.
7. Add fried baingans. Sprinkle ¼ tsp salt and stir gently on low fire for a few minutes till well mixed. Serve hot.

Sukhe Matar Mushroom

Mushroom and peas, studded with diced tomatoes, are tossed in a mouth-watering tomato-flavoured cream.

Serves 4

200 gm mushrooms - each cut into 4" pieces

2 cups shelled peas - boiled in water with a little sugar and salt

2 tomatoes - finely chopped

1 large onion - finely chopped

1 small tomato - cut into 1" pieces

1 tsp salt , ¼ tsp turmeric (*haldi*)

½ tsp garam masala

1 tsp coriander (*dhania*) powder

½ tsp red chilli powder

2 tsp finely chopped ginger, 3 tbsp oil

1 green chilli - chopped, 3-4 tbsp cream

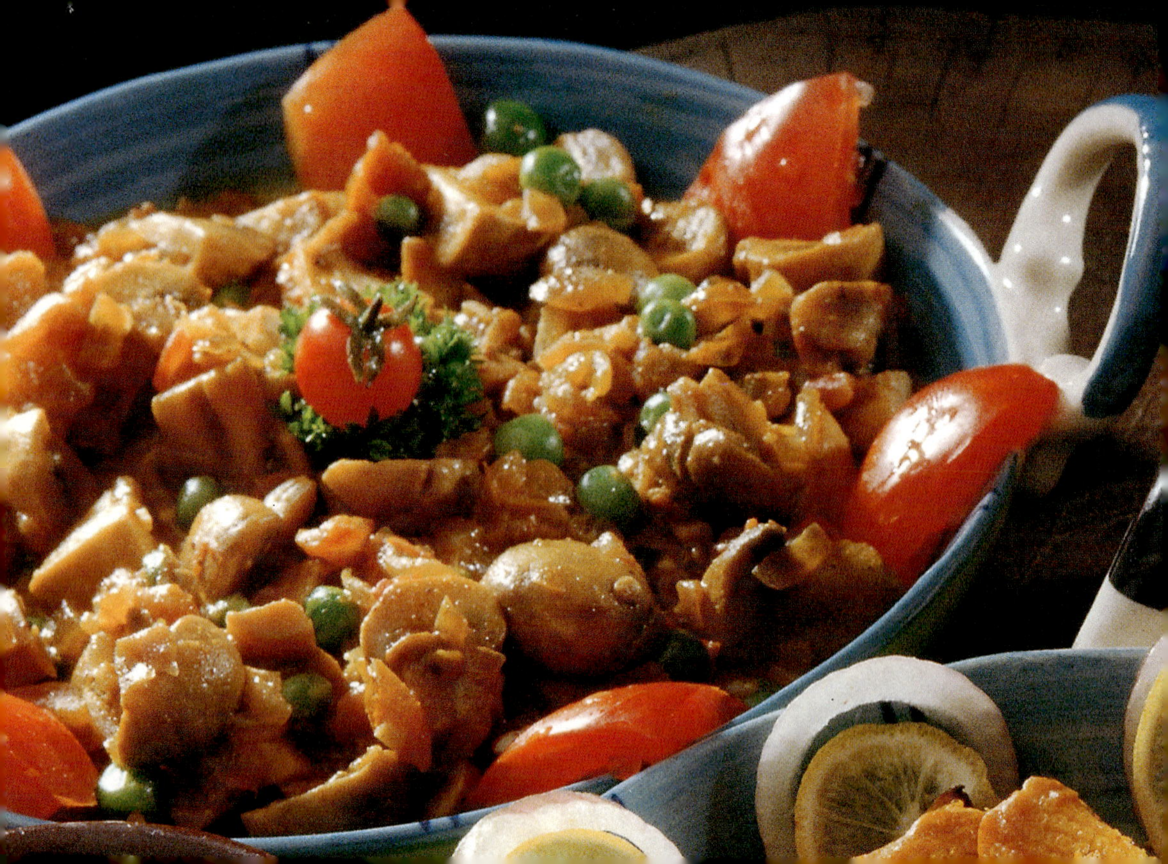

1. Heat 3 tbsp oil. Add onions and stir-fry till soft.
2. Add chopped tomatoes. Stir for 2 minutes.
3. Add mushrooms, stir fry for a minute. Reduce heat. Add salt, haldi, garam masala, dhania powder and red chilli powder. Cook for 5-7 minutes on low heat.
4. Add boiled peas, ginger and green chillies. Keep aside till serving time.
5. At serving time, heat vegetable. Add cream and tomato. Stir for 2 minutes. Serve.

Baked Dishes

Potatoes Baked in Mustard Sauce

Par-boiled, scooped potatoes are generously lathered in a creamy mustard sauce, sprinkled with cheese and baked – good for a hearty family meal and elegant enough for a party.

Serves 4

4 round potatoes - boiled in salted water & peeled

½ cup boiled corn (fresh corn should be boiled with a pinch of *haldi*)

1 tbsp butter, ½ onion - finely chopped, 1 green chilli - deseeded and chopped finely

2 tbsp finely chopped coriander, ¼ tsp salt

¼ tsp freshly ground pepper or to taste, 50 gm cheese

MUSTARD SAUCE

1 tsp mustard powder, 2 tbsp butter, 2 tbsp plain flour (*maida*)

1 bay leaf (*tej patta*), 1½ cups milk, ½ cup cream, ½ tsp salt, or to taste, ¼ tsp pepper

1. Halve the potatoes. Scoop out a little with the back of a teaspoon, leaving a ¼" wall. Sprinkle some salt and pepper on the potatoes. Keep aside.

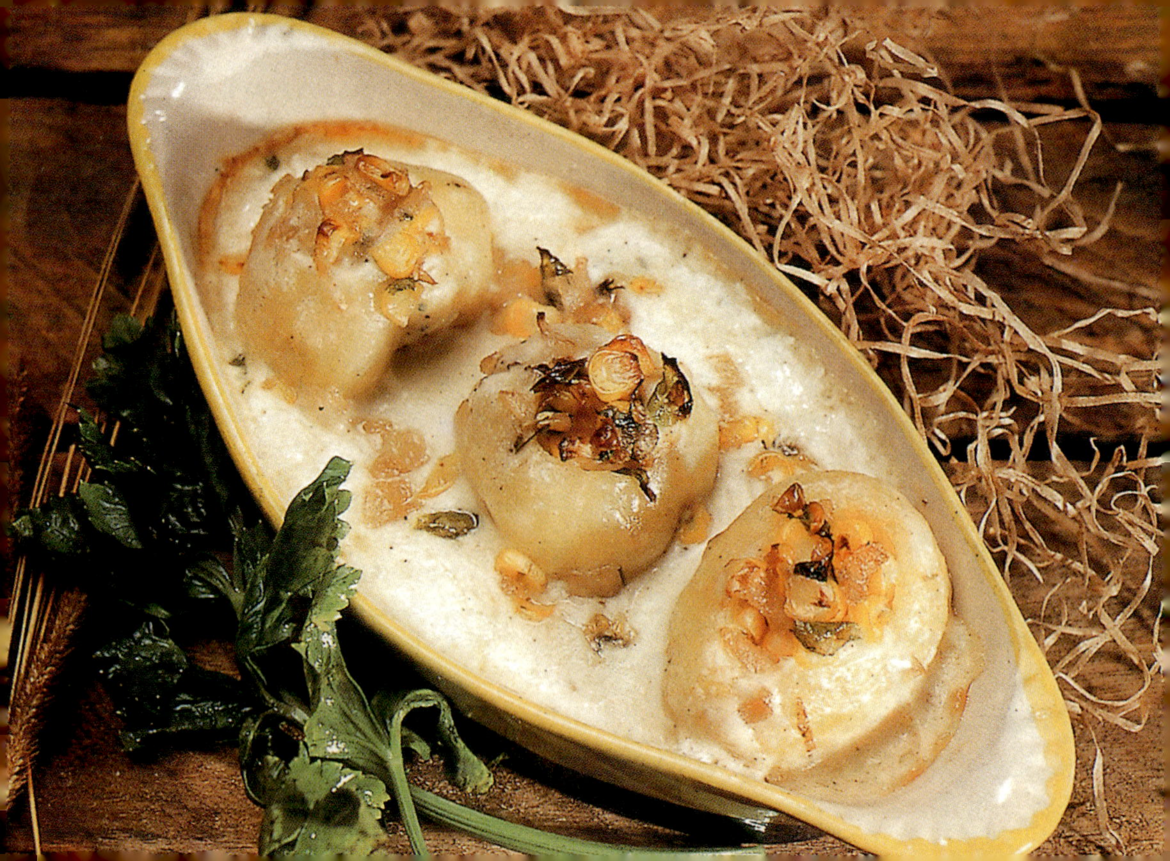

2. Melt 1 tbsp butter in a clean kadhai. Add onion and green chilli. Stir fry till light golden. Add salt, freshly ground pepper & coriander. Add the corn. Toss well for a couple of minutes. Remove from fire.

3. Stuff the filling into the potato shells. Keep the left over filling aside.

4. To prepare the mustard sauce, melt 2 tbsp butter. Add tej patta.

5. Add mustard powder and maida. Cook on low heat for 1 minute.

6. Add milk and mix well. Cook, stirring continuously till the sauce turns slightly thick and coats the back of the spoon.

7. Remove from heat and add the cream. Add salt & pepper to taste. Remove the bay leaf.

8. Pour some mustard sauce (¼ of it) at the base of the serving dish.

9. Slice just a little from the bottom of each stuffed potato, so that it can sit upright in the dish.

10. Arrange the potatoes and spread the rest of the sauce over the potatoes. Sprinkle the left over corn filling. Grate cheese on top and bake till cheese turns brown.

Baked Vegetables

This delicious French-style bake with a golden, cheesy crust frozen mixed vegetables in a coriander-flavoured white sauce.

Serves 5-6

1½ cups mixed vegetables (fresh or frozen)

½ cup grated cheese, optional

some freshly crushed peppercorns

¼ tsp paprika or red chilli flakes

HERBED WHITE SAUCE

2 tbsp butter

2 tbsp plain flour (*maida*)

2 cups milk, ¾ tsp salt

¼ tsp crushed peppercorns

3 tbsp finely chopped cilantro/coriander

¼ tsp grated nutmeg (*jaiphal*)

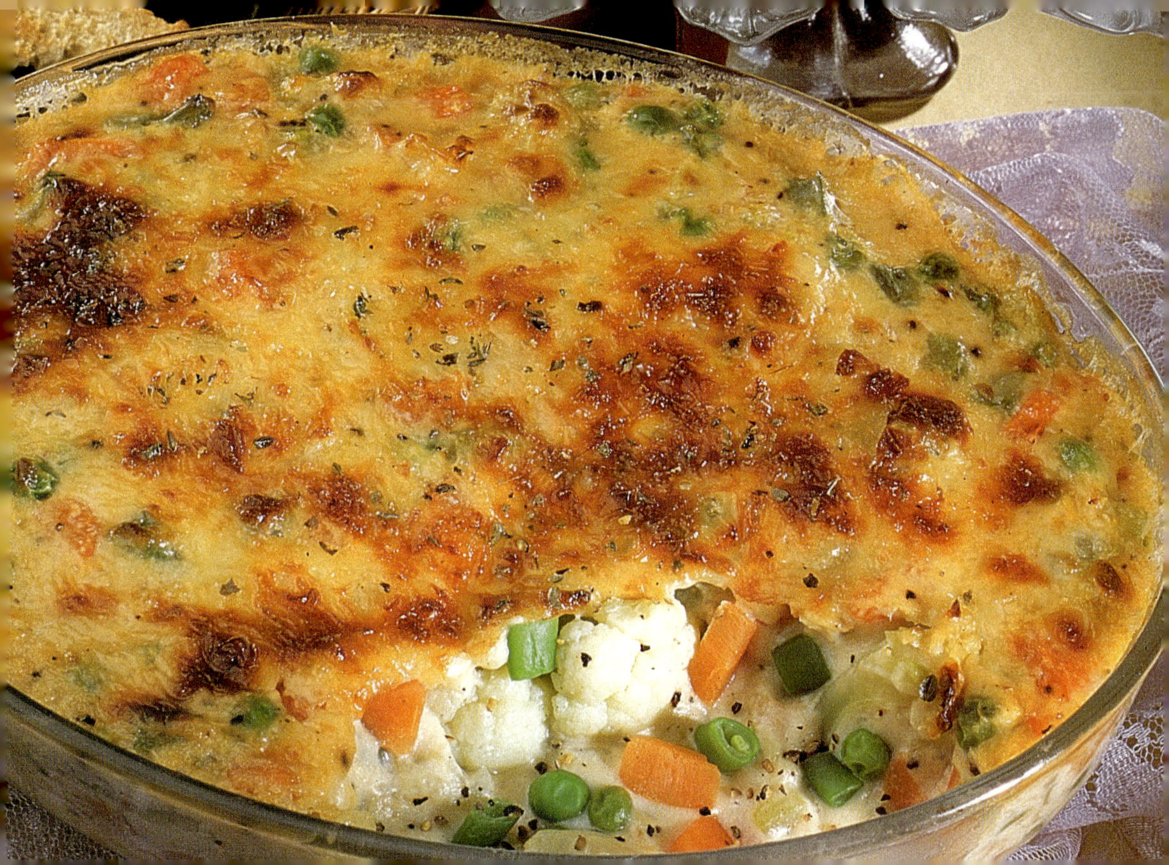

1. To prepare the herbed white sauce, melt 2 tbsp butter in a clean nonstick pan/kadhai. Add cilantro/coriander. Stir for 1 minute. Add flour and cook on low flame for 1-2 minutes. Remove from heat.
2. Add milk, stirring continuously with a whisk. Return to heat. Boil. Simmer for 2 minutes. Add salt, pepper and nutmeg. Stir till a sauce of a coating consistency is ready. Remove from heat.
3. Add half of the cheese to the sauce and mix well.
4. Wash the frozen mixed vegetables. If using fresh, put them in salted boiling water for 2 minutes. Put in a strainer to drain all water. Add vegetables to the sauce. Transfer to a greased baking dish.
5. Sprinkle the remaining cheese on top. Sprinkle some freshly crushed peppercorns and red chilli flakes.
6. Bake in a preheated oven at 180°C/350°F for 20 minutes till golden from the top.

Veggie and Bean Casserole

Pre-cooked ingredients are arranged in a decorative manner then grilled to melt the cheese. This hearty casserole makes a complete meal with some bread.

Serves 8

200 gm mushrooms - cut each into 4

100 gm baby corns - cut into rounds

500 gm spinach

1 cup canned baked beans in sauce

a few drops of tabasco sauce

3 tbsp butter

a pinch of grated nutmeg

1 tsp lemon juice, ½ tsp red chilli flakes

salt & pepper to taste

4 tbsp grated mozzarella cheese

4 tbsp grated cheddar cheese, 1-2 tbsp olive oil

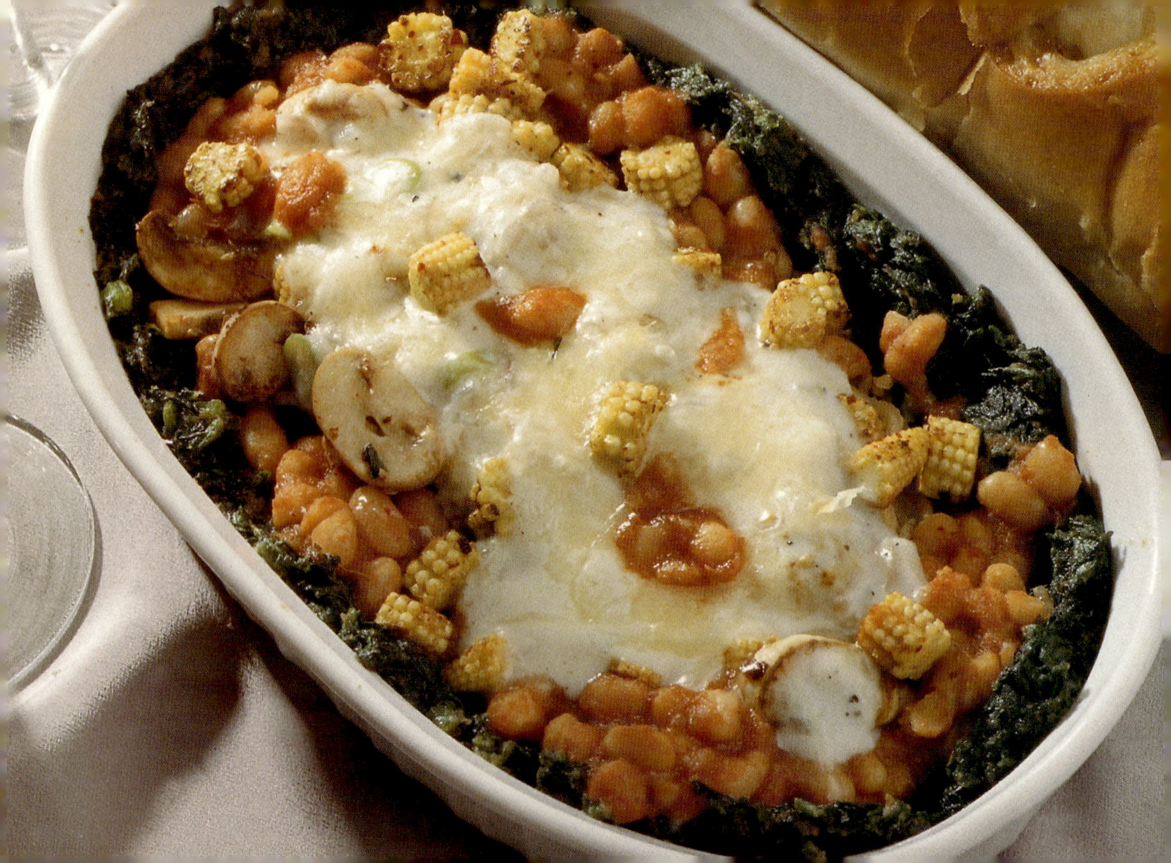

1. Remove the hard stems of the spinach and shred finely. Wash and strain the spinach to drain out all water. Leave the spinach in the strainer for 15 minutes. Pat dry on a kitchen towel.

2. In a pan, add 1 tbsp of butter and cook the spinach till all the water evaporates. Add nutmeg, salt and pepper to taste. Stir fry for 2-3 minutes more till it gets done. Transfer to a shallow, oven proof, glass serving-dish. Spread over the base and a little on the sides too.

3. Mix baked beans with tabasco sauce. Spread a layer of baked beans on spinach, leaving the edges, so that a little spinach shows on the sides.

4. Heat 2 tbsp butter. Add mushrooms and baby corns. Add lemon juice and saute for 5-7 minutes on medium flame till crisp and tender. Add red chilli flakes, salt and pepper to taste.

5. Arrange the baby corns and mushrooms on the baked beans.

6. Mix both the cheeses. Spread on top. Sprinkle some olive oil on the cheese. Put under a grill or microwave for 3 minutes for the cheese to melt. Serve hot.

Stacked Corn Pancakes

Prepare these stacked pancakes in advance. Cut into wedges and garnish with tomato and onion rings. Microwave to allow the cheese to melt into the wholesome corn filling.

Serves 8-10

PANCAKE BATTER (8 PANCAKES)

1½ cups plain flour (*maida*), 2¼ -2½ cups milk

1 tsp salt, ½ tsp pepper, ¼ tsp baking powder

FILLING

2 small onions - cut into rings

1 large capsicum - halved & cut into semi circles to get thin strips

1 cup cooked corn kernels

100-200 gm pizza cheese (a mixture of cheddar and mozzarella cheese)

2 tbsp butter, red chilli powder or crushed red chilli flakes

1. Sift maida and salt. Mix all the other ingredients. Beat well with an eggbeater. Add enough milk to get a pouring consistency.

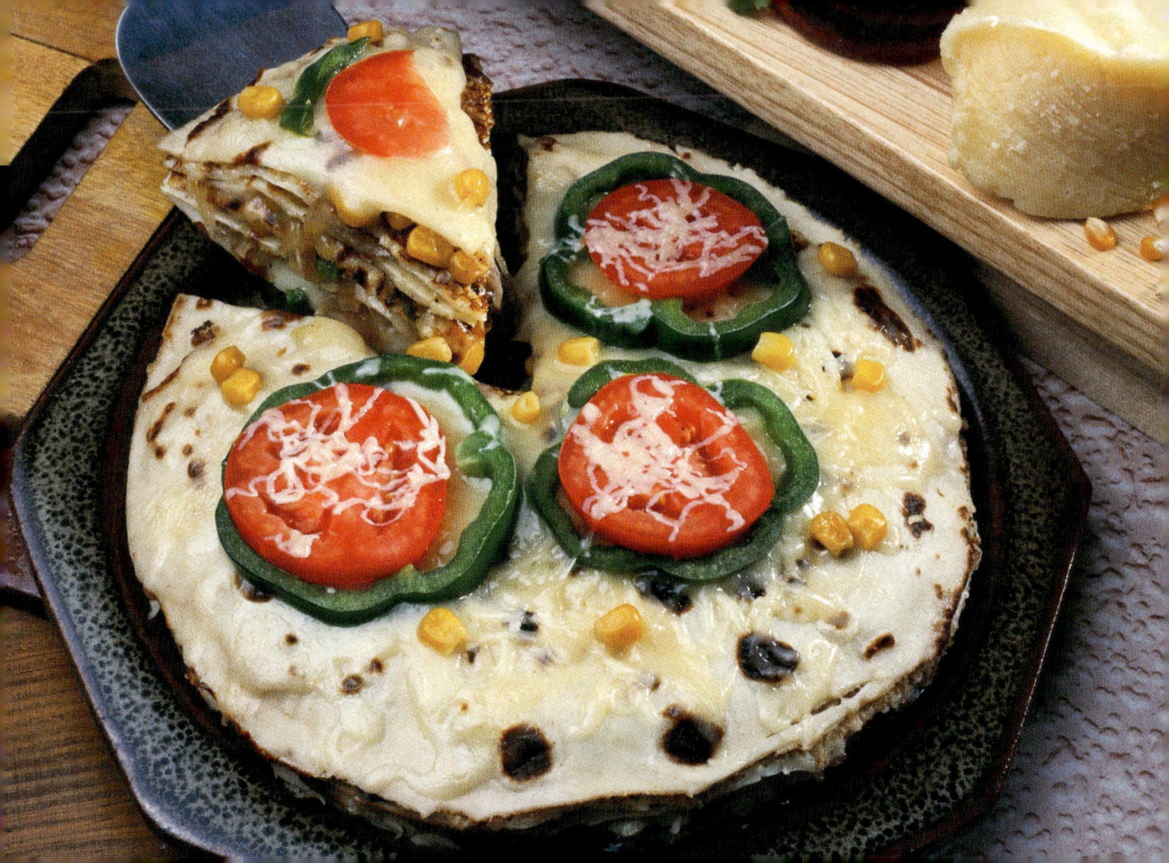

2. Heat a small non-stick frying pan (not too hot). Smear ½ tsp oil on it in the centre. Remove from fire and pour 1/3 cup (1½ big karchi) batter.

3. Tilt the pan to spread the batter to get a slightly thick pancake. Return to fire. Turn the pancake when the under side is cooked. When the other side is cooked, remove from pan. Make 8 such pancakes.

4. Cook onions in butter till light brown. Add red chillies. Add the capsicum. Cook on slow fire for ½ minute.

5. Add corn. Add salt, pepper to taste. Remove from fire.

6. To assemble, place a pancake on a plate. Spread some filling on it. Grate some of the cheese nicely on it all over.

7. Place another pancake and then filling and top the filling with some cheese. End with a pancake.

8. Grate lots of cheese on the top. Garnish with 3 capsicum and 3 tomato rings.

9. Cut into wedges with a sharp pizza cutter, keeping the pieces joined in place. Cover with aluminium foil. Keep aside till serving time. At serving time put in an oven for 10 minutes at 160°C. Serve.

Chinese

American Chopsuey with Sweet & Sour Vegetables

Crisp-fried noodles will absorb sauce and turn limp if mixed with the vegetables too much in advance - so assemble the dish only just before serving for the wonderful crunch.

Serves 4

200 gm noodles

3 tbsp oil, 1 tbsp finely chopped garlic

2 slices tinned pineapple - cut into bite size pieces, ½ cup pineapple syrup

1 onion - sliced, 1 capsicum - cut into thin strips, ½ cup shredded cabbage

8 french beans or snow peas, 4-5 florets cauliflower and 1 carrot - cut into pieces and all vegetables blanched in boiling water for 2 minutes till crisp tender

1½ cups water mixed with 1 vegetable soup cube

½ tsp white pepper OR ¼ tsp pepper, ½ tsp salt, or to taste, 4 tsp sugar

¼ tsp ajinomoto (optional), 1 tsp soya sauce, ¼ cup white vinegar

¼ cup tomato ketchup, 3 tbsp cornflour dissolved in ¼ cup water

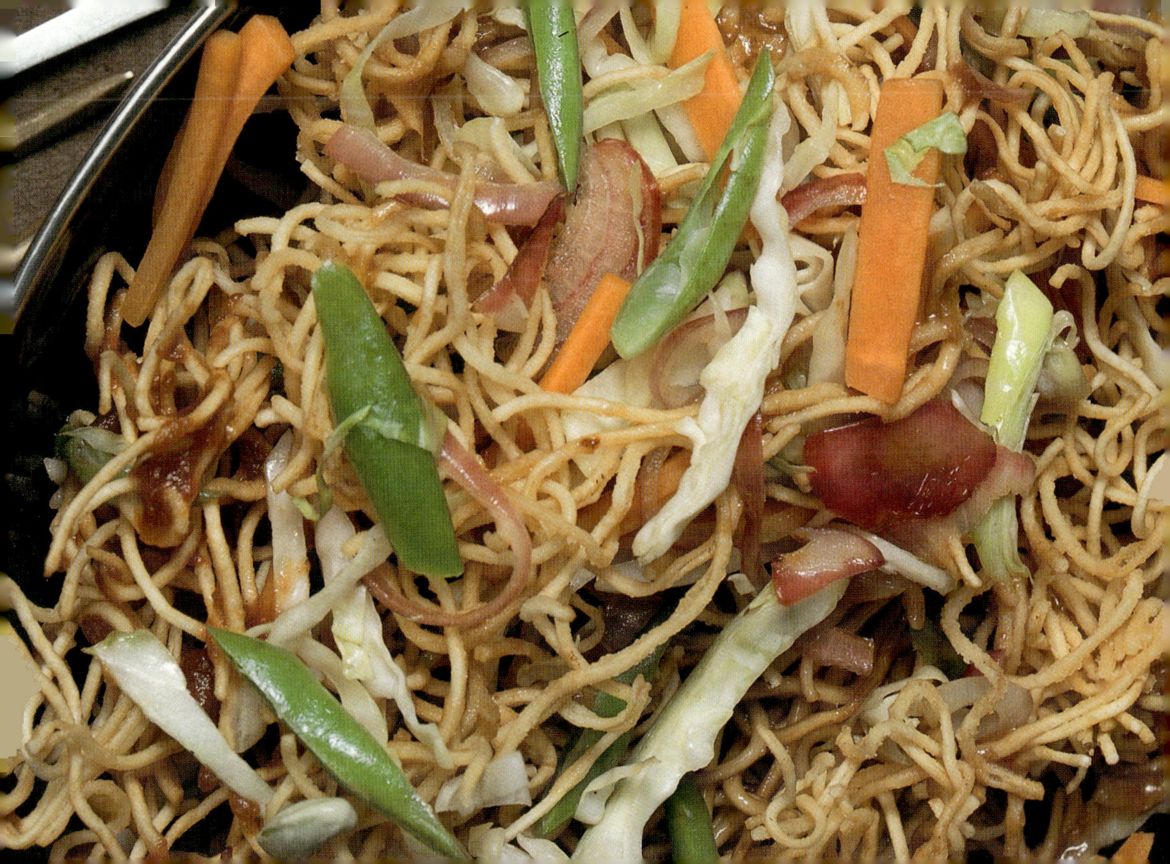

1. To boil noodles, boil 8-10 cups water with 2 tsp salt and 1 tbsp oil. Add noodles to boiling water. Stir with a fork. Remove from fire. Let noodles be in hot water for 1 minute. Strain. Sprinkle 1 tbsp oil and mix lightly. Spread in a tray. Let them cool. To prepare crispy noodles, sprinkle 2 tbsp cornflour on boiled noodles to absorb any excess water. Keep aside. Heat oil in a medium kadhai or wok. Put half of the noodles together to form a nest. Fry till light golden and crisp. Remove from oil and fry the remaining half of the noodles. If the kadhai is small, fry in 3-4 batches. Let them cool. Store them in an air tight box till serving time.

2. Heat 3 tbsp of oil. Add garlic and onion. Stir for 1 minute.

3. Add cabbage and capsicum. Stir fry on high heat for 1 minute. Add blanched carrots, beans and cauliflower. Stir for a minute. Add water mixed with a soup cube. Add pineapple syrup. Bring to a boil. Add salt, pepper, ajinomoto, soya sauce, vinegar, sugar and tomato ketchup. Add pineapple.

4. Add cornflour paste, stirring continuously. Cook for about 2 minutes, till thick.

5. To serve, spread crispy noodles on a serving platter, keeping aside a few for the top. Top with the prepared vegetables. Sprinkle some left over crispy noodles on it. Serve hot.

Cottage Cheese in Hot Garlic Sauce

Batter-fried paneer adds texture to this complex sauce – serve with rice to all garlic lovers!

Serves 3-4

200 gm cottage cheese (*paneer*) or tofu

BATTER

3 tbsp cornflour, 3 tbsp plain flour (*maida*), 1 tsp soya sauce

½ tsp garlic or ginger paste, ¼ tsp each of pepper & salt, ¼ cup water

GARLIC SAUCE

20 flakes garlic - chopped & crushed roughly in a small spice grinder (1½ tbsp)

2 dry, red chillies - broken into two, deseeded and chopped with a knife or scissors

½ onion - chopped, 1 capsicum - cut into tiny cubes, 3 tbsp oil

4 tbsp tomato ketchup, 2 tsp red chilli sauce, 2 tsp soya sauce, ½ tsp pepper

1 tsp salt, a pinch sugar, 2 tsp vinegar

1½ cups water, 3½ tbsp cornflour mixed with ½ cup water

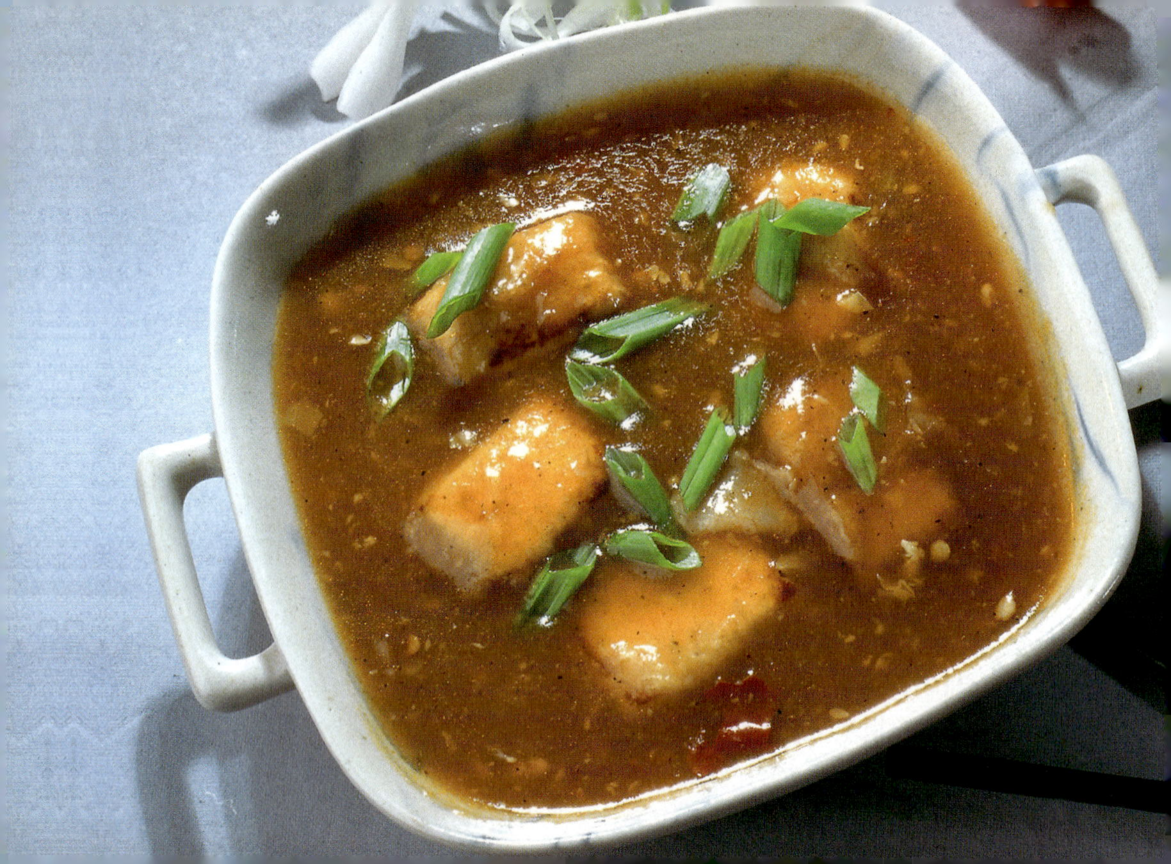

1. To prepare the sauce, peel and grind the garlic to a very rough paste in a small grinder. Keep the mixer on just for 1-2 seconds. Do not make a smooth paste.

2. Heat 3 tbsp oil. Remove from fire. Add garlic and red chilli bits. Stir till garlic starts to change its colour.

3. Add onion, cook till soft.

4. Add tomato ketchup, red chilli sauce, soya sauce, pepper and salt. Cook for 1 minute on low heat. Add sugar and vinegar.

5. Add capsicum. Add water, give one boil.

6. Add cornflour paste, stirring all the time. Cook for 2 minutes on low heat. Remove from heat. Keep sauce aside.

7. Cut tofu or paneer into 1" cubes.

8. Make a thick coating batter by mixing all ingredients of the batter with a little water.

9. Dip tofu or paneer pieces and deep fry to a golden colour. Keep aside.

10. At serving time, add fried paneer/tofu to sauce and boil for 2 minutes. Serve with rice.

Stir-fried Beans with Tofu/Paneer

This recipe uses green beans and paneer fingers for an easy-to-make stir-fry, but any bouquet of seasonal vegetables may be used.

Serves 4

200 gm French beans or snow peas

50-75 gm tofu/paneer - cut into thin, 2" long pieces

1 onion, 4 tbsp oil

1½" piece ginger - cut into jullienes or thin match sticks (1½ tbsp)

3-4 green chillies - shredded (cut into thin pieces lengthwise)

OTHER INGREDIENTS

1½ tbsp soya sauce, 2½ tbsp tomato ketchup

1 tbsp vinegar, 1 tsp red chilli sauce

2 tbsp sherry or wine (optional)

1½ tbsp worcester sauce, ½ tsp salt, ¼ tsp pepper, or to taste

½ tsp ajinomoto (optional), 1 tbsp dry bread crumbs (optional)

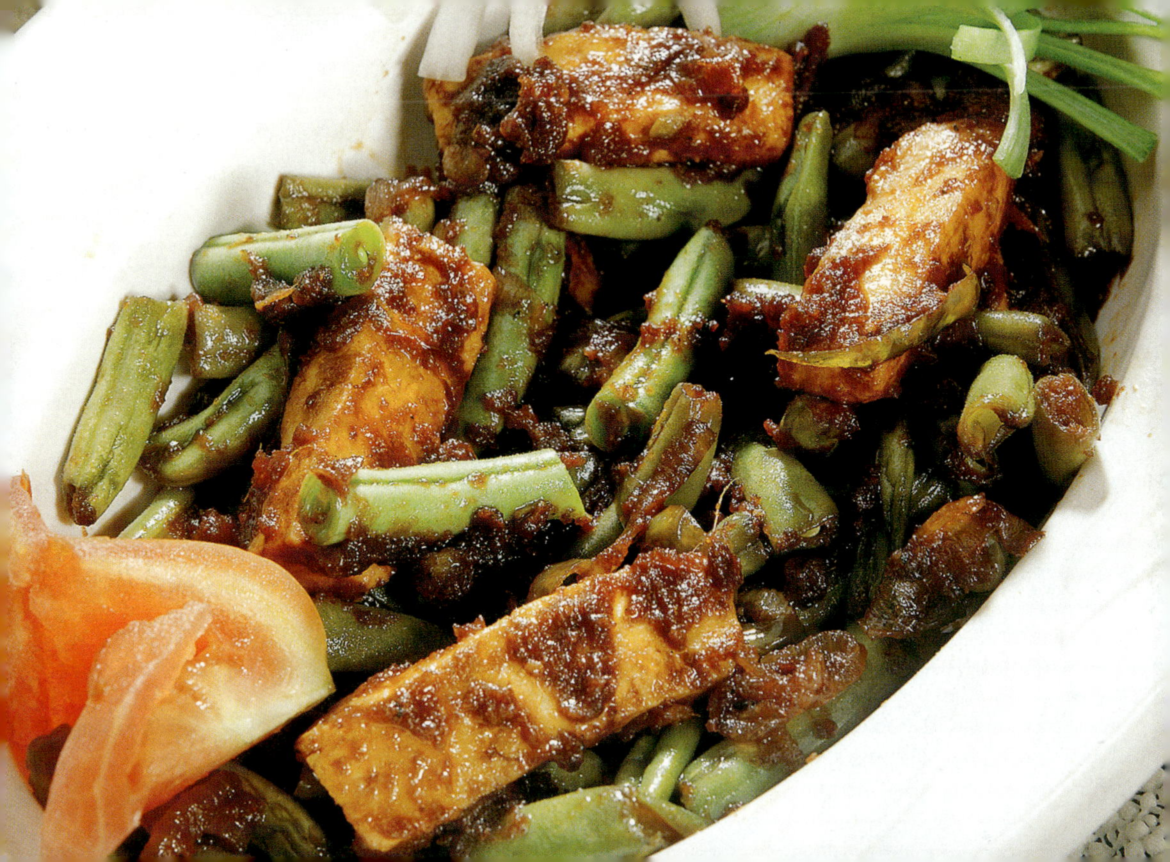

1. Remove strings/threads from snow peas or beans.
2. If using snow peas, keep whole. If using french beans, cut each into 1½-2" pieces. If using beans, boil 4-5 cups water with 1 tsp salt and 1 tsp sugar. Add beans and boil for 1-2 minutes. Strain.
3. Peel onion. Cut into half and then cut widthwise to get half rings, which when opened become thin long strips and you get shredded onion.
4. Heat 4 tbsp oil in pan. Add onion, cook till golden.
5. Add ginger jullienes and green chillies. Stir-fry for 1-2 minutes till ginger turns golden.
6. Add snow peas or beans and stir fry for 3-4 minutes till vegetable turns crisp-tender. Keep the vegetable spread out in the pan while stir frying.
7. Reduce heat. Add soya sauce, tomato ketchup, vinegar, red chilli sauce, sherry, worcester sauce, salt, pepper and ajinomoto.
8. Add paneer and mix well.
9. Add bread crumbs. Stir fry on low heat for 2 minutes till the vegetable blends well with the sauces. Serve hot.

Haka Noodles

Sprouts, bamboo shoots, cabbage and other vegetables are seasoned with garlic, red chillies, soya sauce and vinegar – add to basic noodles and you have the winning combination!

Serves 4

STIR FRIED NOODLES

200 gm haka noodles, 2 tbsp oil

3 dry whole red chillies - broken into bits

½ tsp chilli powder, 2 tsp soya sauce, ½ tsp salt

VEGETABLES

1 capsicum - shredded, 1 carrot - shredded, ½ cup shredded cabbage, 3 tbsp oil

3-4 flakes garlic crushed and chopped - optional, 2-3 spring onions or 1 ordinary onion

2 tbsp shredded bamboo shoots - optional, 3-4 tbsp bean sprouts - optional

1-2 tbsp dried mushrooms, ½ tsp each of salt & pepper, ½ tsp sugar

½ tsp ajinomoto (optional), 1 tbsp soya sauce, 2 tsp vinegar, 1 cup water

1½ tbsp cornflour dissolved in ½ cup water

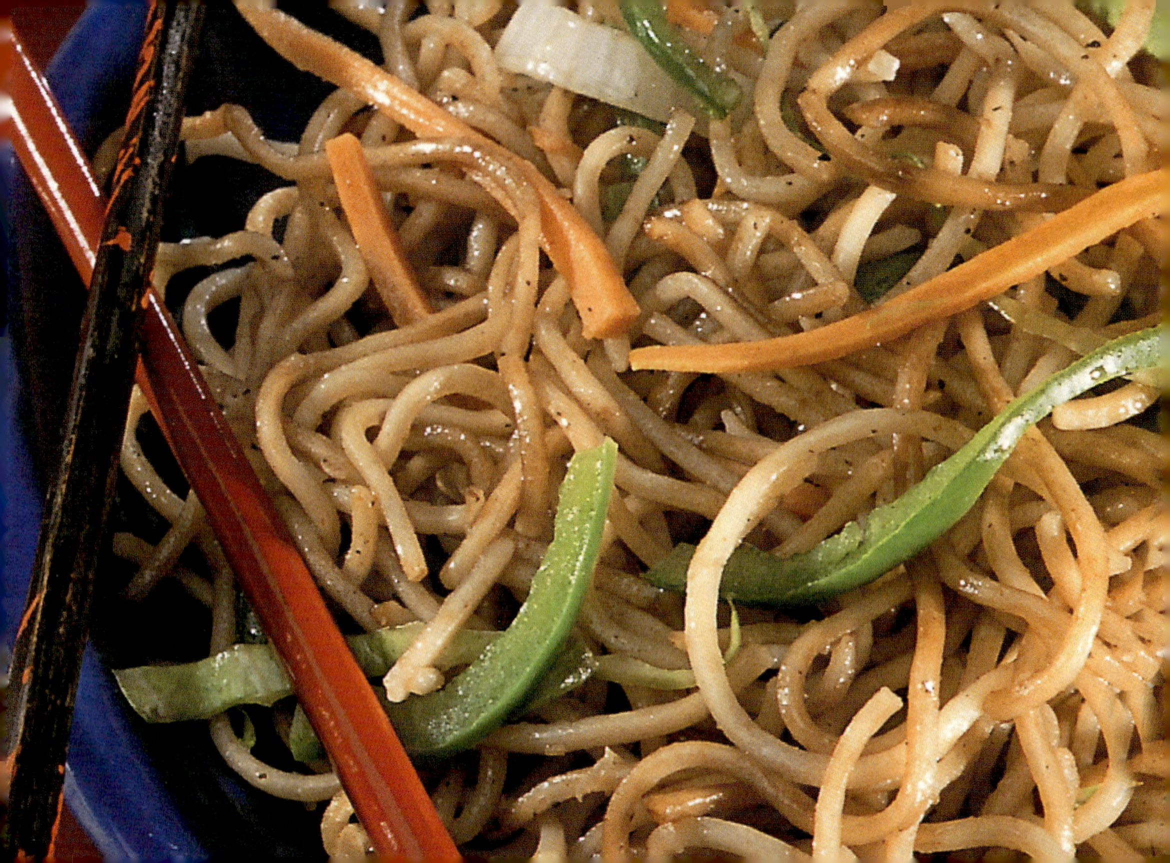

1. To boil noodles, boil 8-10 cups water with 2 tsp salt and 1 tbsp oil. Add noodles to boiling water. Stir with a fork. Remove from fire. Let noodles be in hot water for 2 minutes or till almost done. Strain. Sprinkle 1 tbsp oil and mix lightly. Spread in a tray. Leave aside for 30 minutes.

2. Heat 3 tbsp oil. Remove from fire, add broken red chillies and chilli powder.

3. Return to fire & mix in the boiled noodles, salt and soya sauce. Fry for 1 minute, till the noodles turn brown. Keep the fried noodles aside.

4. To prepare the vegetables, shred all vegetables. Heat 3 tbsp oil. Reduce heat and add garlic. Cook for ½ minute.

5. Add vegetables in sequence of their tenderness - onions, sprouts, bamboo shoots, capsicum, carrot and cabbage.

6. Add ajinomoto, salt and pepper. Add soya sauce and vinegar. Cook for ½ minute.

7. Add water. Boil. Add cornflour paste, stirring continuously. Cook for 1 minute till thick. Remove from fire. To serve, spread the fried noodles on a platter. Pour the prepared hot vegetables over the noodles.

Peanut Fried Rice

Shredded green onions and roasted peanuts add a jazzy tone to this cheerful rice dish!

Serves 3-4

1½ cups uncooked rice

3 tbsp oil, 4 flakes garlic - crushed (optional)

2 green chillies - chopped finely

2 green onions - chopped till the greens, keep greens separate

1 tsp salt, 1 tsp pepper, ½ tsp soya sauce (according to the colour desired)

1 tsp vinegar (optional), ½ tsp tomato ketchup

GRIND TOGETHER TO A PASTE

3 tbsp roasted peanuts (*moongphali*)

5½ tbsp milk

FOR GARNISHING

2 tbsp roasted peanuts - roughly crushed on a chakla belan

1. In a large pan, boil 8-10 cups water with 2 tsp salt and 1 tbsp oil. Add rice to boiling water.
2. Cook uncovered, on high flame for about 7-8 minutes only. Stir once in between.
3. Remove from fire before they get overcooked. Drain.
4. Spread on a large tray and keep aside for them to cool down completely.
5. Grind all ingredients of paste to a smooth paste.
6. Chop spring onions till the greens, keep white and green separately.
7. Heat oil. Stir fry garlic, green chillies and white of onions.
8. Add peanut paste. Mix. Reduce heat, add salt, pepper, soya sauce, vinegar and tomato ketchup. Mix.
9. Add boiled rice and green portion of spring onions. Mix and stir fry the rice for 2 minutes with the help of 2 forks. Remove from fire.
10. Serve hot garnished with crushed roasted peanuts.

Chilli Cauliflower

Break the ice at your next party with these hot, sweet and spicy, batter-fried florets!

Serves 2-3

1 small flower of cauliflower (*gobhi*)

1½ tbsp flour (*maida*), 1½ tbsp cornflour, ½ tsp salt

1-1½ tbsp soya sauce, 2½ tbsp chilli sauce, 5 tbsp tomato sauce, 1 tbsp vinegar

4-5 green chillies - slit lengthwise, 6 flakes of crushed garlic - optional

3 tbsp chopped coriander, ¼ tsp sugar, ½ tsp salt, ½ tsp pepper

1. Mix flour, cornflour and salt. Add enough water, about 3 tbsp, to make a batter of a thick pouring consistency, such that it coats the cauliflower.

2. Cut gobhi into small florets. Dip each piece in the batter and deep fry to a golden brown colour on medium heat.

3. Heat 2 tbsp oil. Fry the green chillies and garlic. Reduce heat. Add salt, pepper and sugar. Add soya sauce, chilli sauce, tomato sauce and vinegar. Stir.

4. Add the fried gobhi and coriander. Mix well. Check salt and pepper. Serve hot. A toothpick may be inserted in each piece to serve it as a snack.

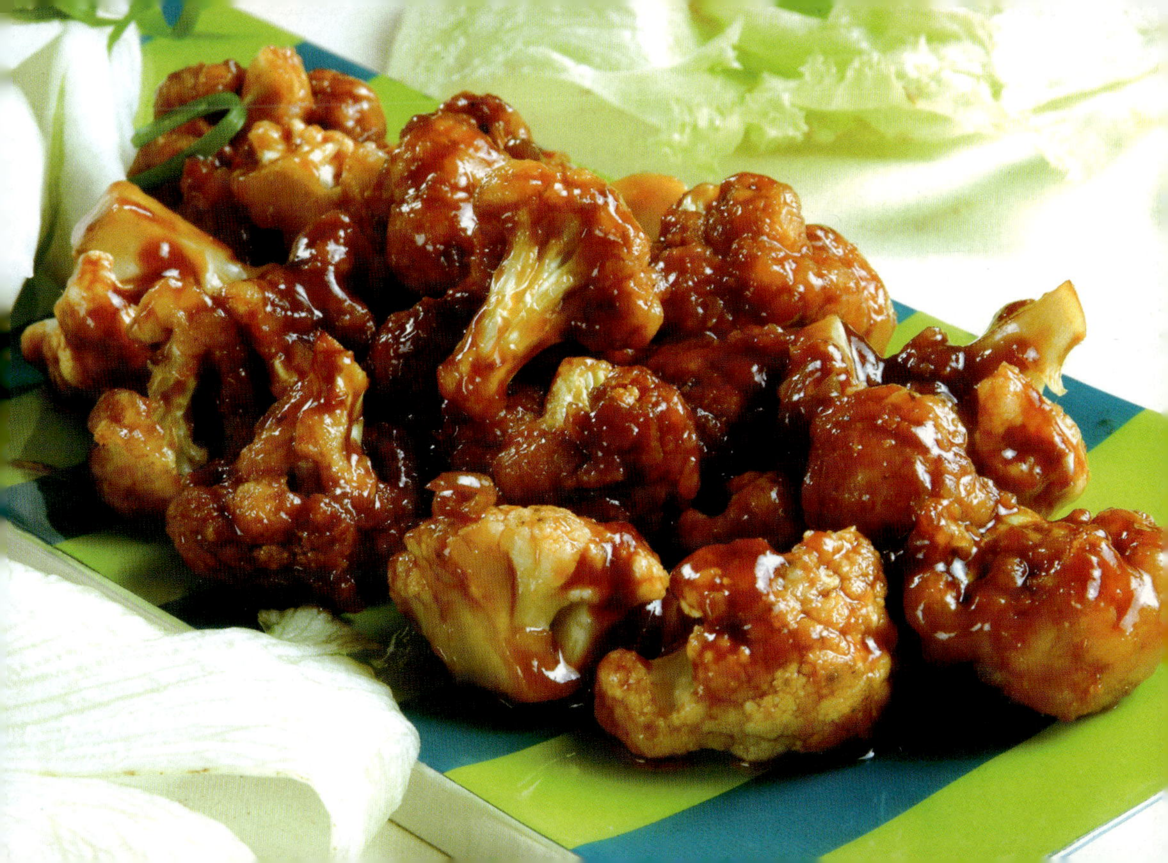

Snacks

Super Veggie Pizza

Pizza base, topped with crunchy onions, black olives, sweet corn, spicy jalapenos or pickled green chillies and melted cheese, drizzled with olive oil.

Makes 2

2 ready-made pizza base

TOMATO SAUCE

250 gm (3) tomatoes - blanched (put in hot water and peeled) and chopped finely

½ cup ready-made tomato puree, 4-5 flakes garlic - crushed

1 tsp dried oregano, 1 tsp vinegar, salt and freshly ground pepper to taste, 1 tsp oil

TOPPING

1 onion - cut into half and then cut into thin rounds to get semi circles

1 capsicum - cut into 4 and then cut thinly widthwise to get thin strips

½ cup tinned corn kernels or cooked fresh corn or thinly sliced baby corns

a few slices of pickled jalapenos or pickled green chillies

10-15 black or green olives - cut into slices, 200 gm mozzarella or pizza cheese - grated

1-2 tbsp olive oil

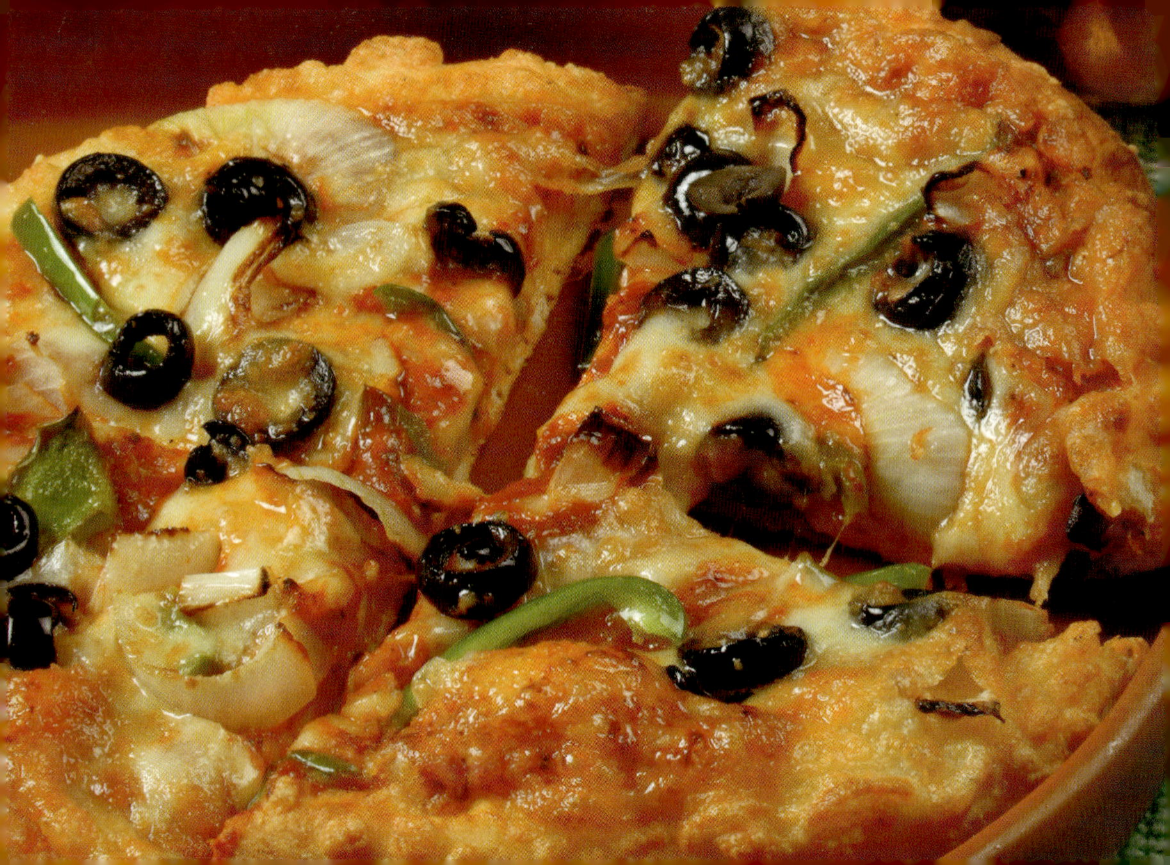

1. For the tomato sauce, heat oil in a pan. Add garlic. Stir and immediately add all other ingredients of the sauce. Bring to a boil. Lower heat and simmer on low heat for 7-8 minutes, stirring occasionally until it is reduced in quantity and thick enough to spread without being runny. Remove sauce from fire.
2. Place pizza base on a rack.
3. Spread 1 tbsp melted butter or olive oil over each pizza base, covering the edges.
4. Spoon some tomato sauce over pizza base, leaving ½" all around the edges.
5. Sprinkle some grated cheese on each base.
6. Sprinkle onions. Sprinkle some capsicum, corn and jalapenos too.
7. Sprinkle left over mozzarella cheese. Arrange olives. Drizzle some olive oil.
8. Bake at 180°C (350°F) for 15 minutes until golden and crisp. Serve hot.

Pan-Fried Chinese Tikkas

Learn how to give a barbecue-charred look to sophisticated paneer and capsicum tikkas made in a non-stick pan on the stove top.

Makes 16

250 gm paneer - cut into 1" squares of ½" thickness

2-3 tbsp oil

1 green capsicum - cut into ¾" cubes

MARINADE

½ cup thick curd (*dahi*) - keep in a strainer for 15 minutes

1 tbsp cornflour

1½ tsp soya sauce

1 tsp tomato ketchup

¾ tsp salt, or to taste

¼ tsp black pepper

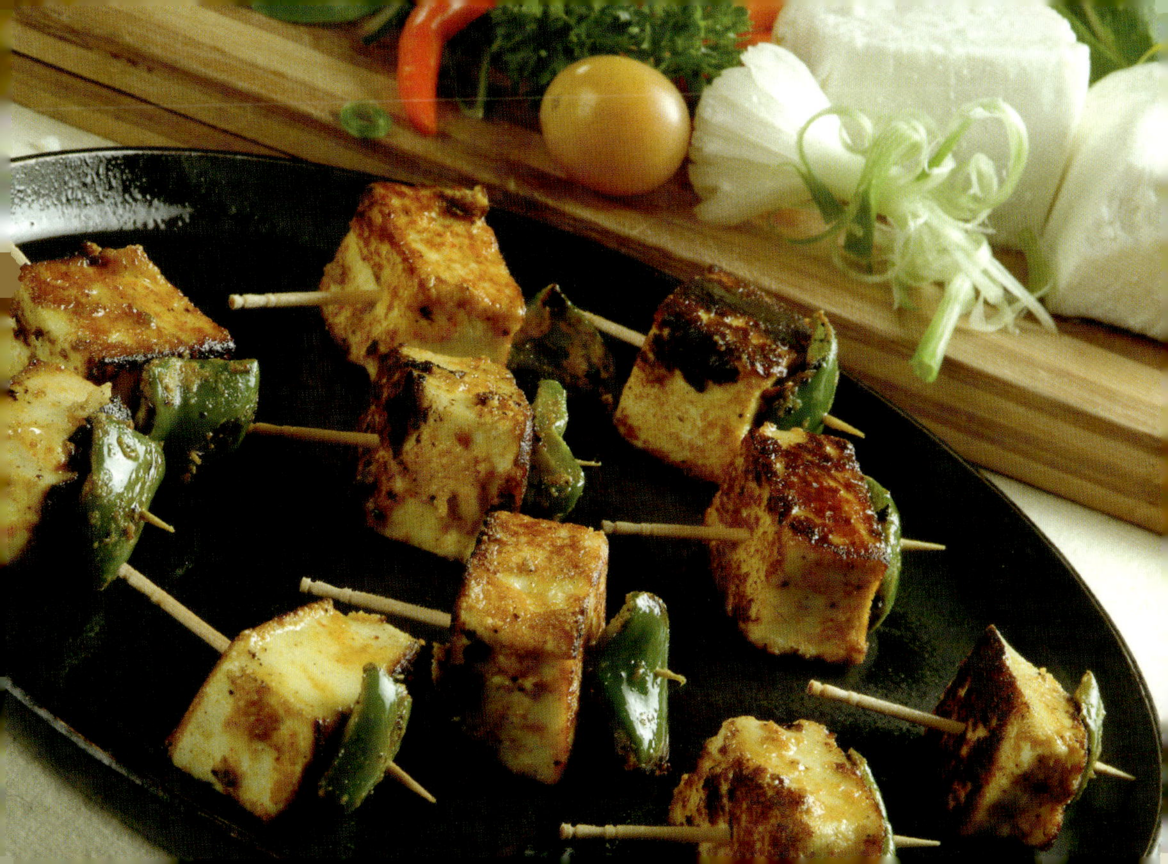

1. Mix thick dahi with all the other ingredients of the marinade and marinate paneer in it. Keep aside in the fridge till serving time.

2. At the time of serving, heat a non stick pan. Spread 2 tbsp oil on it. Pick-up the paneer pieces from the marinade and place on the pan in a single layer. Cook both sides for 1-2 minutes on medium heat till the marinade thickens and clings to the pieces. Be careful while sauteing the pieces as they tend to burn very fast. Transfer to a serving platter.

3. Add the capsicum to the remaining marinade. Mix well. Stir the capsicum cubes in the pan for 2 minutes on medium heat. Sprinkle some salt, pepper, ½ tsp each of soya sauce and tomato ketchup too on the capsicum.

4. Place a capsicum cube on a piece of paneer. Pierce both with a toothpick and serve hot.

Note: While sauteing the capsicum, it is better if they are not stirred too frequently. Leaving one side on the hot pan for sometime gives them a slight charred look.

Matar Makhane ke Kebab

Makes 8 kebabs

1 cup boiled or frozen shelled peas (*matar*)

1 cup puffed lotus seeds (*makhanas*)

1 tbsp oil

2 green chillies - chopped

2-3 tbsp cashewnuts

¾ tsp salt or to taste

½ tsp pepper

¼ tsp garam masala

seeds of 4-5 green cardamoms (*chhoti elaichi*)

chaat masala

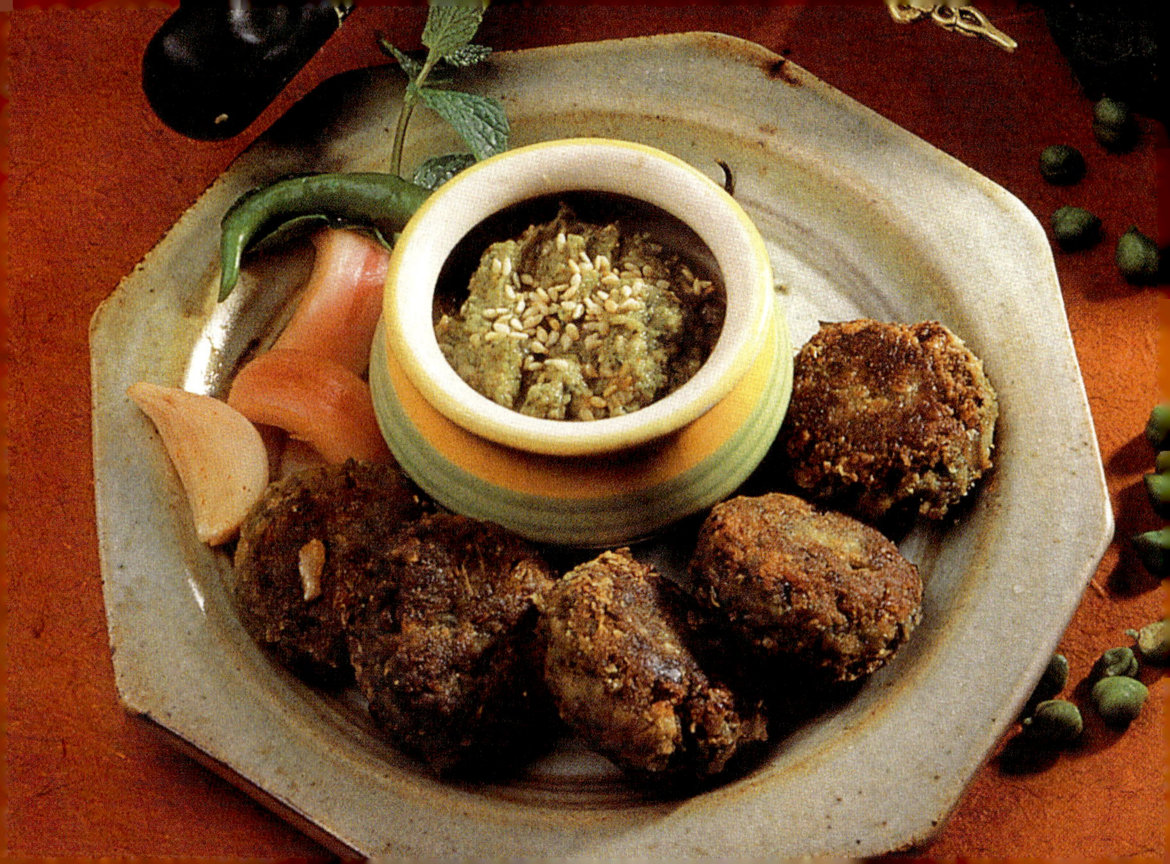

1. Heat 1 tbsp oil in kadhai. Add makhanas and saute for 3-4 minutes.
2. Add cashewnuts and saute till cashews start changing colour. Remove makhanas and cashewnuts from the kadhai.
3. In the same kadhai (without any oil leftover), add peas and saute for 2 minutes. Remove peas from kadhai.
4. Grind makhanas and cashewnuts together to a rough powder.
5. Grind peas with green chillies to a fine paste.
6. Mix makhanas and pea paste. Add salt, pepper, garam masala and chhoti elaichi.
7. Makes small balls and flatten them to get small round kebabs (tikkis).
8. Shallow fry on tawa or pan in 1-2 tbsp oil till brown and crisp.
9. Sprinkle chaat masala and serve hot.

Palak Pakoras

Serves 4-5

24 palak (spinach) leaves, with 2" long stems

BATTER

½ cup chick pea flour (*besan*), ¼ cup semolina (*suji*)

½ tsp carom seeds (*ajwain*), ½ tsp salt, ¼ tsp red chilli powder

½ tsp ground coriander (*dhania powder*), ¾ cup water or as required, oil to deep-fry

1. Take spinach leaves including a little stem of about 2". Wash the spinach and pat dry on a clean kitchen towel.

2. Put all the ingredients for the batter in a bowl, adding water to make a thick batter with a coating consistency. Do not make it thin as it will not coat the leaves properly.

3. Heat the oil in a wok. Dip each spinach leaf in batter so that it gets well coated.

4. Fry the leaves on medium heat, a few at a time, till golden and crisp on both sides. Remove and drain on absorbent paper towels. Serve immediately.

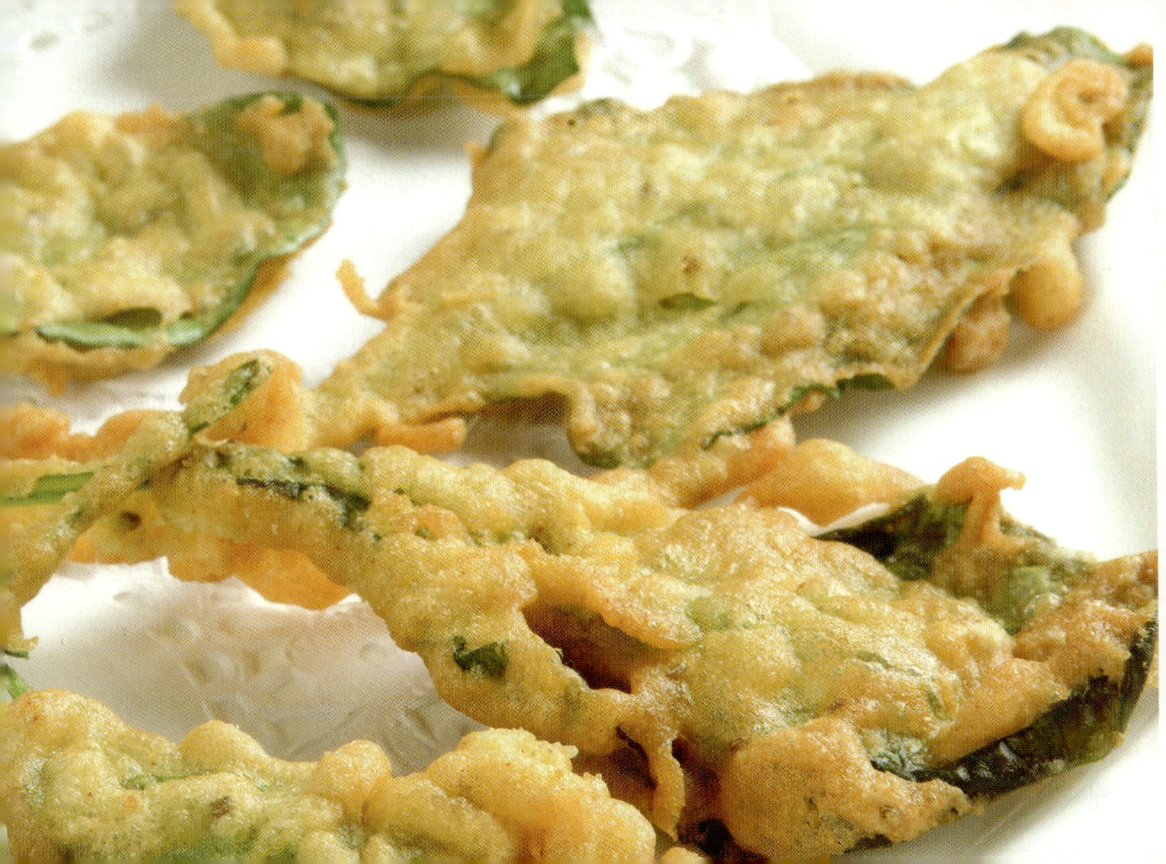

Pasta in Quick Tomato Sauce

Serves 4

3 cups unboiled penne or any other shape pasta - boiled

2 medium green or coloured capsicums - cut into strips, 3 tbsp oil

2 tsp crushed garlic, 1 cup ready-made tomato puree, ¾ tsp pepper, 1 tsp oregano

1½ tsp salt, 1 cup milk or ½ cup milk & ½ cup cream

1. Heat 1 tbsp oil in a non stick pan, add ½ tsp garlic, wait for ½ minute. Add boiled pasta, saute for 1-2 minutes. Add ¼ tsp pepper and ½ tsp oregano. Mix, remove pasta from the pan and keep aside.

2. In the same pan heat 2 tbsp oil. Add 1½ tsp crushed garlic. Wait till it changes colour. Add ready-made tomato puree. Cook for 3-4 minutes, till oil separates.

3. Add ½ tsp pepper, ½ tsp oregano and 1½ tsp salt. Mix. Reduce heat and cook for 2 minutes. Add boiled pasta, mix well. Keep aside.

4. At serving time, return the pasta on fire. Add capsicum and milk or milk and cream. Mix well. Add little water if needed. Check salt and pepper. Remove from fire. Serve hot with garlic bread.

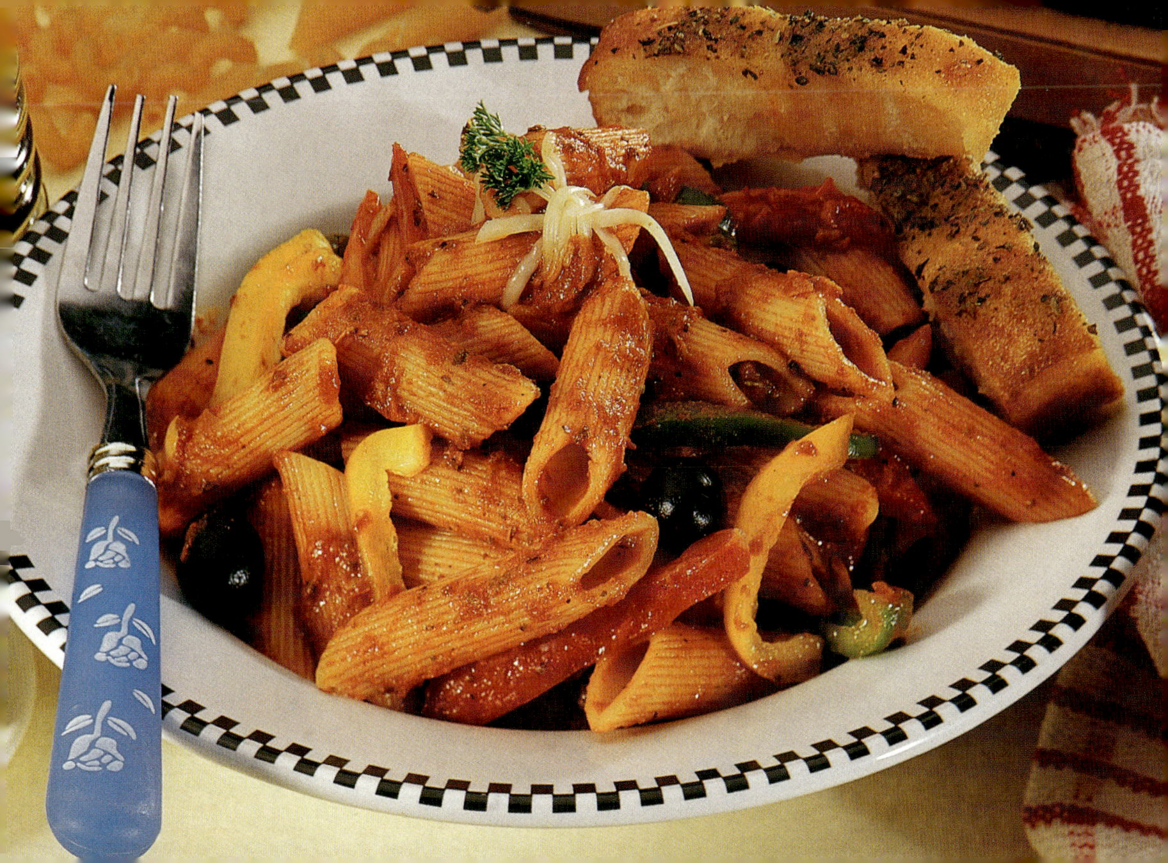

Tikka Parantha Sandwich

This is an amazing construction of roomali roti folded into a square packet and fried. The surprise filling is marinated, sautéed paneer lathered with a thick, hot, green chutney.

Makes 4

400 gm paneer - cut into 1" pieces of ½" thickness, 1 small capsicum - chopped
4 *roomali rotis* or thin large *maida-atta rotis*, 1 large onion - cut into semi circles
chaat masala to sprinkle
hari dahi poodina chutney - recipe given below, some desi ghee or butter to spread

MARINADE

1 cup curd (*dahi*) - hang in a muslin cloth for 15 minutes and squeezed
2 tbsp finely chopped coriander, ½ tsp cumin seeds (*jeera*) powder, ½ tsp garam masala
½ tsp chaat masala, ¼ tsp black salt (*kala namak*), 1 tsp red chilli powder, 1 tsp salt
½ tsp turmeric (*haldi*), 1 tsp ginger paste, 1 tsp garlic paste

ROOMALI ROTI

1½ cups plain flour (*maida*), 1 cup whole wheat flour (*atta*), 2 tbsp oil
½ tsp salt - knead to a dough, 1 tbsp ghee, ½ tbsp plain flour (*maida*) - make a paste

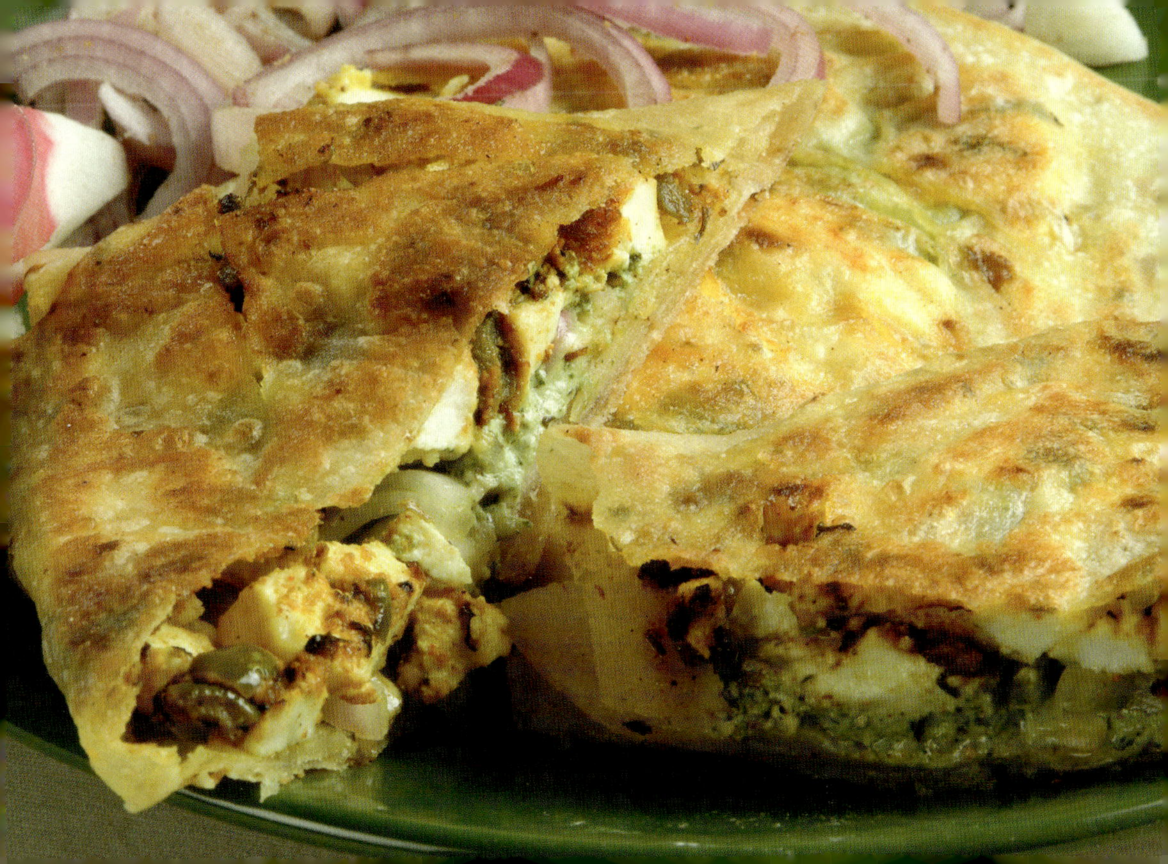

DAHI POODINA CHUTNEY (GRIND TOGETHER)

½ cup mint (*poodina*), ½ cup green coriander (*hara dhania*), 2 green chillies, ½ onion
2 flakes garlic, 1 cup curd - hang for 15 minutes, 1 tsp oil, 1 tsp lemon juice, or to taste
a pinch of black salt (*kala namak*), ¼ tsp roated cumin seeds (*bhuna jeera*), salt to taste

1. Hang dahi (curd) in a muslin cloth for 15 minutes.

2. Mix all ingredients of marinade in a bowl. Mix well Add paneer and capsicum. Keep aside for 15 minutes.

3. For the chutney, grind poodina, dhania, green chillies, onion and garlic to a green paste. Beat hung curd till smooth. Add green paste to it. Add all the other ingredients. Keep aside.

4. Heat 1 tbsp oil in a pan, add marinated paneer and capsicum. Cook on low heat for 5-6 minutes or till dry and golden brown from both sides.

5. To make roomali rotis, roll out 2 small pooris with small balls of the dough. Stick together with 1 tsp paste. Roll out to a big roti. Cook quickly on a hot tawa without browning. Remove from tawa and separate the two rotis. Fold like a roomal (hankey) and keep in a casserole.

6. On a roti, spread some melted butter or desi ghee. Put ¼ of the paneer tikka mixture in the centre. Crumble the pieces lightly. Throw some onion slices on it. Sprinkle some chat masala.

7. Sprinkle just 1 tbsp hari chutney on the onions.

8. Fold the right and left sides and the other 2 sides also to get a square.

9. Put some ghee or butter on a tawa and fry on both sides till crisp. Cut into 4 pieces. Serve hot.

Desserts

Bread and Paneer Pudding

In this innovative interpretation of a traditional dessert, fried bread is soaked in a mixture of sweetened, thickened milk cooked with grated paneer.

Serves 8-10

6 slices of bread - sides removed and each cut into 4 pieces & deep fried till golden brown

5 tbsp of chopped mixed nuts (*badaam, kishmish, pista* etc.), ¾ cup cold milk

PANEER LAYER

4 cups milk

¾ cup sugar, ¾ tsp green cardamom (*chhoti elaichi*) powdered

8 tsp cornflour dissolved in ½ cup milk

100 gm cottage cheese (*paneer*) - grated

2 drops of *kewra* essence

1. For the paneer layer, boil 4 cups milk. Simmer on low flame for 20 minutes.

2. In the meanwhile, boil sugar with ½ cup water in a separate pan. Keep on low heat for 5 minutes. Add grated paneer. Cook for 1 minute. Remove from fire.

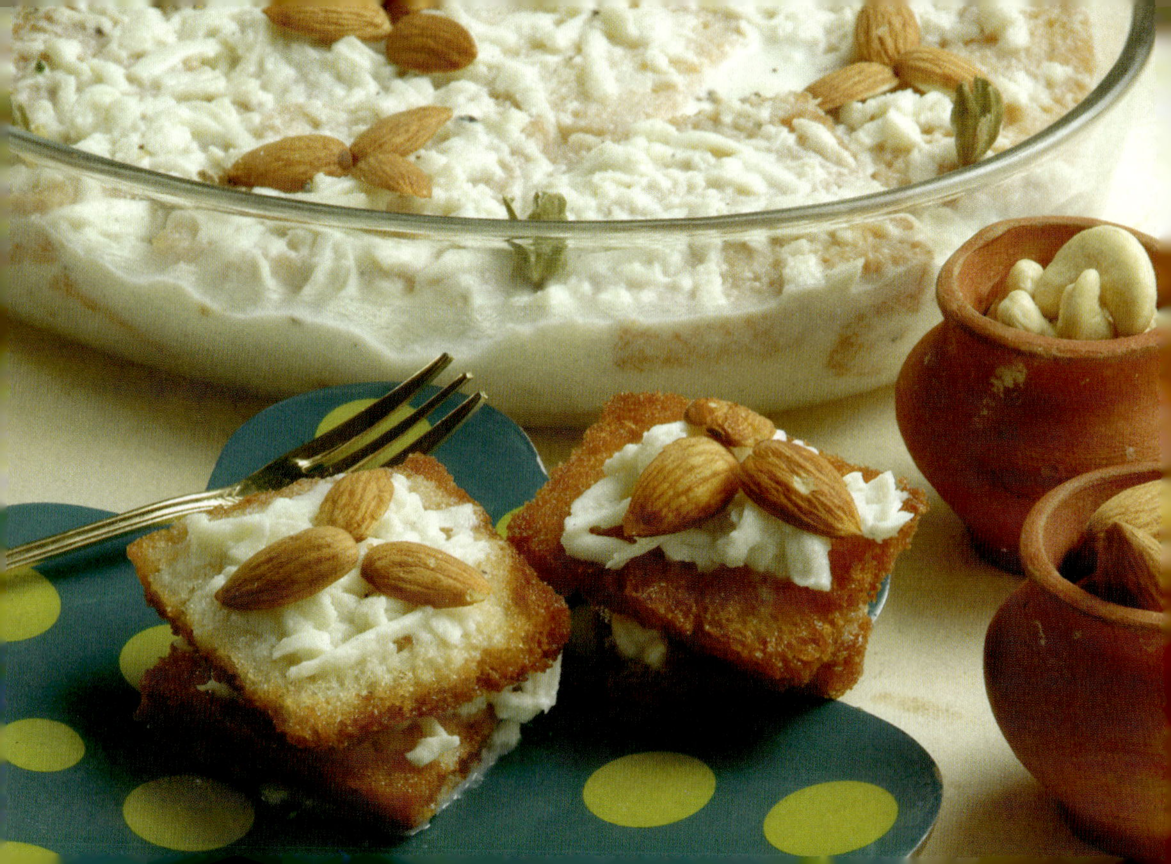

3. Add cornflour paste to the milk of step 1, stirring continuously. Keep stirring for 2 minutes till thick. Add the prepared sugar & paneer mixture. Boil. Keep on heat for 1 minute. Remove from fire. Cool. Add essence. Sprinkle elaichi powder.

4. Remove the side crusts of bread. Cut each slice into 4 square pieces. This way you get 24 small pieces of bread. Heat oil in a kadhai. Deep fry each piece till golden brown. Let it cool.

5. Dip each piece of bread for a second in some cold milk, put in a small flat dish. Remove immediately.

6. Take a serving dish. Spread 1 tbsp of paneer layer at the bottom of the dish. Place pieces of fried bread together in a single layer to cover the base of the dish.

7. Spread about ½ tsp of the paneer mixture on each piece. Sprinkle 1 tbsp of chopped mixed nuts on the paneer.

8. Repeat the bread layer in the same way with bread pieces first then the paneer layer and finally topped with 1½ tbsp of chopped mixed nuts.

9. Repeat with the left over bread, paneer and nuts to get a 3 layered pudding. Cover with a cling wrap (plastic film) and let it set for at least ½ hour before serving. Serve at room temperature.

Mango Kulfi

Stack your freezer with this all-time favourite – luscious mango-cream scented with cardamom and studded with pistachio nuts.

Makes 8

1 large mango chopped (1½ cups)

6½ cups milk, 7 tbsp sugar, seeds of 3-4 green cardamom (*chhoti elaichi*) - crushed

2 tbsp cornflour mixed with ½ cup milk, 8-10 pistas - blanched & chopped, ½ cup fresh cream

1. Keeping ½ cup chopped mango aside, puree the rest of the mango (1 cup) with ½ cup milk in a mixer.

2. Boil 6 cups milk with sugar and elaichi for about 20 minutes on low heat till it is reduced to about ½ quantity, about 3 cups.

3. Add cornflour paste stirring continuously. Stir for 5 minutes on low heat. Remove from fire and let the milk cool.

4. Add mango puree to thickened milk. Mix well. Add finely chopped mango pieces and finely chopped pistas also. Add cream. Mix well. Pour into kulfi moulds and freeze for 5-6 hours or overnight.

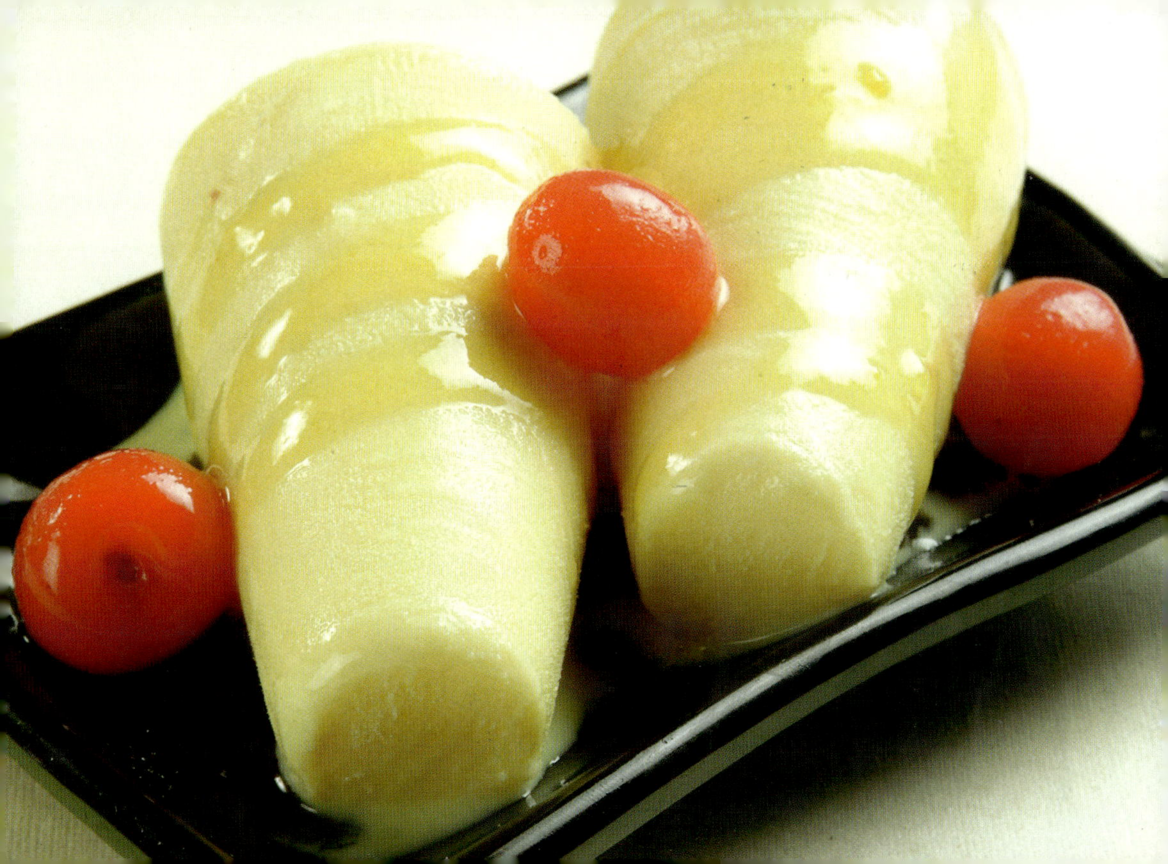

Glossary of Names/Terms

HINDI OR ENGLISH NAMES as used in India	USED IN USA/UK/OTHER COUNTRIES
Baingan	Eggplant, aubergine
Bhutta	Corn
Capsicum	Bell peppers
Chhoti Elaichi	Green cardamom
Chilli powder	Red chilli powder, Cayenne pepper
Cornflour	Cornstarch
Cream	Heavy whipping cream
Dalchini	Cinnamon
French beans	Green beans
Gobhi	Cauliflower
Hara Dhania	Cilantro/fresh or green coriander
Hari Gobhi	Broccoli
Hari Mirch	Green hot peppers, green chillies
Imli	Tamarind
Jeera	Cumin seeds
Saunf	Fennel
Soda bicarb	Baking soda
Til	Sesame seeds

INTERNATIONAL CONVERSION GUIDE

These are not exact equivalents; they've been rounded-off to make measuring easier.

WEIGHTS & MEASURES

METRIC	IMPERIAL
15 g	½ oz
30 g	1 oz
60 g	2 oz
90 g	3 oz
125 g	4 oz (¼ lb)
155 g	5 oz
185 g	6 oz
220 g	7 oz
250 g	8 oz (½ lb)
280 g	9 oz
315 g	10 oz
345 g	11 oz
375 g	12 oz (¾ lb)
410 g	13 oz
440 g	14 oz
470 g	15 oz
500 g	16 oz (1 lb)
750 g	24 oz (1½ lb)
1 kg	30 oz (2 lb)

LIQUID MEASURES

METRIC	IMPERIAL
30 ml	1 fluid oz
60 ml	2 fluid oz
100 ml	3 fluid oz
125 ml	4 fluid oz
150 ml	5 fluid oz (¼ pint/1 gill)
190 ml	6 fluid oz
250 ml	8 fluid oz
300 ml	10 fluid oz (½ pint)
500 ml	16 fluid oz
600 ml	20 fluid oz (1 pint)
1000 ml	1¾ pints

CUPS & SPOON MEASURES

METRIC	IMPERIAL
1 ml	¼ tsp
2 ml	½ tsp
5 ml	1 tsp
15 ml	1 tbsp
60 ml	¼ cup
125 ml	½ cup
250 ml	1 cup

HELPFUL MEASURES

METRIC	IMPERIAL
3 mm	1/8 in
6 mm	¼ in
1 cm	½ in
2 cm	¾ in
2.5 cm	1 in
5 cm	2 in
6 cm	2½ in
8 cm	3 in
10 cm	4 in
13 cm	5 in
15 cm	6 in
18 cm	7 in
20 cm	8 in
23 cm	9 in
25 cm	10 in
28 cm	11 in
30 cm	12 in (1 ft)

HOW TO MEASURE

When using the graduated metric measuring cups, it is important to shake the dry ingredients loosely into the required cup. Do not tap the cup on the table, or pack the ingredients into the cup unless otherwise directed. Level top of cup with a knife. When using graduated metric measuring spoons, level top of spoon with a knife. When measuring liquids in the jug, place jug on a flat surface, check for accuracy at eye level.

OVEN TEMPERATURE

These oven temperatures are only a guide. Always check the manufacturer's manual.

	°C (Celsius)	°F (Fahrenheit)	Gas Mark
Very low	120	250	1
Low	150	300	2
Moderately low	160	325	3
Moderate	180	350	4
Moderately high	190	375	5
High	200	400	6
Very high	230	450	7